INFERNO

INFERNO

The Firebombing of Japan
March 9–August 15, 1945

Edwin P. Hoyt

MADISON BOOKS

Lanham • New York • Oxford

Published by Madison Books
4720 Boston Way
Lanham, Maryland 20706

12 Hid's Copse Road
Cumnor Hill, Oxford OX2 9JJ, England

Distributed by National Book Network

Library of Congress Cataloging-in-Publication Data

Hoyt, Edwin Palmer.
    Inferno : the firebombing of Japan, March 9–August 15, 1945 / Edwin P. Hoyt.
        p. cm.
    Includes bibliographical references.
    ISBN 1-56833-149-5
    1. World War, 1939–1945—Aerial operations, American.   2. Bombing,
Aerial—Japan.   3. Incendiary bombs—History—20th century.   4. World War,
1939–1945—Japan.   I. Title.
    D790+
    940.54'25—dc21   00-027131

Contents

Acknowledgments

This book has been fifteen years in the making. I conceived an idea for a book about the World War II firebombing of Japan in 1984 and in 1986 traveled to Japan to do research. Under the pseudonym Hoito Edoin (My name in Japanese) I wrote *The Night Tokyo Burned* (New York: St. Martin's Press, 1987). It did not get a great deal of attention, because at that time very few people in the United States were interested in genocide and crimes against humanity.

In recent years that concern has grown, fueled by atrocities in Bosnia, Africa, Iraq, Indonesia, and most recently in Kosovo. Also, I am now convinced, I was mistaken to put the emphasis on the U.S. XX Air Force and General Curtis LeMay, who conceived of the idea of burning up Japan "to shorten the war." The emphasis should have been where it is in this book, on the horrors of holocaust.

I am indebted to a number of people for materials in this book. Seiichi Soeda of the Japan Foreign Press Center arranged the itinerary for my trip around Japan to Nagoya, Osaka, and Kobe, and occasionally acted as my interpreter in Tokyo. Yoko Asakawa and Hiroko Hattori also interpreted for me.

Katsumoto Saotome was living in Mukojima, Tokyo, during the great air raid of March 10, 1945. He and his family escaped injury, and their house was not burned down. He later wrote a number of books about the bombing of Japan. I interviewed him in Tokyo.

Masatake Obata was a fire warden in Tokyo on the night of March 10, 1945. His wife and four children were killed in the firestorm. Firebombs exploded almost at his feet, tumbling him into the air and causing burns over his entire body—burns so severe that doctors refused to treat him and sent him to the morgue to die. He survived the first few days without food or water, on willpower alone, before he was recognized by his mother and saved. After the war he turned his business over to his brothers and devoted the rest of his life to the cause of citizens wounded in the air raids and to the establishment of an Air Raid Memorial Museum. I interviewed him in the summer of 1986.

Chisako Sugiyama of Nagoya was working in the anatomy section of Nanzan University at the time of the first fire raid on Nagoya, on March 12. She lost the sight in her left eye. After the war she became chairwoman of the National Liaison Committee for Citizens Wounded in the Air Raids. I interviewed her in August 1986 in Nagoya.

Dr. Hitoshi Koyama of Osaka was fourteen years old when Osaka was firebombed. He survived to become professor of Japanese literature at Kansai University and author of a book on the firebombing of Osaka: *The Osaka Great Air Raids* (Osaka: Toufu Shuppan, 1985). I interviewed him in Osaka in August 1986.

Shigeharu Kobayashi of Osaka was a police inspector in the intelligence section of the Osaka Prefectural Police in the summer of 1945. I interviewed him about the air raids in the summer of 1986.

Takako Iga of Osaka was a high school student at the time of the Osaka fire raids. She lost her mother and younger brother, but survived with her father. She was badly burned and still bore the scars forty years later when I interviewed her. She was then chairwoman of the Osaka committee for Citizens Wounded in the Air Raids.

Masahisa Kimimoto was sixteen years old at the time of the Kobe fire raids. He survived and later produced a movie on the Kobe air raids.

Kimiko Mikitani was a homemaker in Kobe during the bombing. She was badly injured and lost her infant son to the fire dragon when he was swept off her back by a gust of wind while she was crossing the Dai Wada Bridge. She was a member of the Group to Record Air Raids on Kobe when I interviewed her in the summer of 1986.

Hanako Kanai of Tokyo was a schoolgirl at the time of the great fire raid. She later included the story in her published reminiscences. I interviewed her at the Fukagawa No. 1 Middle School in Tokyo in August 1986.

I am indebted to many librarians in Japan for research assistance, including those at The National Library (Diet); Japan Foreign Press Center; Tokyo Koto Public Library, Koto Ku, Tokyo; International House, Tokyo; Nagoya

Municipal Museum; Osaka Shakai Fukushi Kaikan; Kobe City Central Library; *Chunichi Shimbun* and *The Japan Times*; and Librarian Deon Grinnell of the U.S. Air Force base at Yokota. Also, Yvonne Kinkaid of the USAF history program arranged for me to have an important book on the strategic bombing program.

Foreword

In the history of World War II two things stand out. One could not call them events, because they occupied more time than that word signifies. They were policies, the results of decisions made by the authorities of Germany and the United States. They are:

The Holocaust, in which the Nazis killed six million Jews and other ethnic groups deemed "undesirable."

The U.S. government's firebombing of Japan, in which more than two million Japanese lost their property, 300,000 civilians were killed and 500,000 civilians were wounded.

Both policies, by the standards of the late twentieth and early twenty-first centuries, are war crimes.

In the summer of 1998, a U.N. commission meeting in Rome passed a treaty to establish the International Criminal Court at The Hague, the Netherlands. The approval—120 for and 7 against—was overwhelming.

The United States was one of the seven nations that voted against establishing the court. Also casting negative votes were China, which is presently occupying Tibet; Israel, which has forcibly moved populations about, an indictable offense under the treaty; Iraq, whose treatment of minorities is indictable; and Libya, India, and Mexico. The affirmative votes for the treaty represented a rebuke to the United States, which is regarded by many countries as a bully who insists on playing under his own rules. The main U.S. objection was the creation of an independent prosecutor. The United States also wanted Americans to be exempt from universal jurisdiction.

The commission rejected the U.S. positions because of the Clinton administration's lack of credibility. For example, the United States has not rejoined the International Court of Justice, decades after withdrawing, because that court ruled the mining of Nicaraguan harbors in peacetime as illegal.

The International Criminal Court will be able to try anyone, anywhere for crimes against humanity. If Americans are charged, the United States will have to persuade every veto holder on the Security Council to vote to dismiss the case. As an example of what could go wrong, U.S. officials say that actions could be brought against the U.S. peacekeeping force in Korea. But critics aver that the U.S. objection is more far-reaching; that the establishment of the court jeopardizes the position of the United States as a superpower that is above international law.

This view is supported by the blithe rejection by Washington of complaints about the 1998 bombing of a pharmaceutical factory in Khartoum, Sudan, on the premise (unproven) that it was part of an international terrorist conspiracy. Former U.S. president Jimmy Carter's call for an investigation of the bombing was also rejected by the Clinton White House. It is conceivable that this case could still be brought to the International Criminal Court.

Several times since the end of World War II, the United States has intervened in the affairs of other nations. One most flagrant attempt was an attempt to destroy the North Korean government in retaliation for that country's attack on the Republic of Korea in 1951. The U.S. effort, led by General Douglas MacArthur under the cloak of the United Nations, came to naught when China intervened and fought the war to a stalemate.

The most recent intervention has been in the form of NATO's campaign in Yugoslavia to force President Slobodan Milosevic to accept a NATO-imposed peace plan that would give the people of Kosovo independence in three years.

Kosovo is setting a new standard for international intervention that extends beyond the U.N. Charter and far beyond the principle, sacrosanct until recently, that no government should intervene in the domestic affairs of another state. What the NATO powers have said now is that a nation's performance on human rights supersedes its right to sovereignty. "We are building toward world legal order," said Jane Holl, director of the Carnegie Commission on the Prevention of Deadly Violence.

Perhaps, but the United States is dragging its feet, and reminding the world that it is the single superpower and self-appointed police officer of the world.

In the past decade much has changed in the world. New treaties and ethnic crises in many areas (Tibet and Kosovo, for example) have brought about sweeping revisions in law and policy. At the top of the list is the antigenocide convention, which dates back to 1948. The United States did not sign it until 1986 and it was not until two years later that then-President Ronald Reagan signed a law making genocide a crime in the United States. The humanitarian principles embodied in that convention prompted the U.S. military interventions in Somalia, Bosnia, Haiti, and on behalf of Kurdish refugees in northern Iraq.

All the more reason to be perplexed about the U.S. rejection of the treaty to establish the International Criminal Court. One can only assume that this rejection represents another aspect of the two-faced American attitude toward law: one law for the United States, and one law for the rest of the world.

The purpose of the International Criminal Court is to assure that serious crimes against humanity do not go unpunished. After World War II, the Allies attempted to establish international justice in the Nuremberg and Tokyo War Crime Trials. What they produced, it is generally acknowledged half a century later, was nothing more than "victor's justice." To have produced real justice, the victors' war crimes as well as those of the vanquished would have had to be addressed; they were not.

Principal among those Allied excesses were the destruction of Dresden and the firebombing of Japan. If these occurred today, the perpetrating government leaders could be brought before the International Criminal Court. They might go unpunished, as they did in fact half a century ago. But the military leaders would have had to defend themselves against the serious charges of crimes against civilians. The vanquished would have had their day in court.

In 1999 NATO engineered an indictment against Yugoslav President Milosevic for war crimes. But the war crimes in NATO's war against Serbia were not all on the Serbian side. NATO's targeting of civilians for bombing, as attested by Spanish airmen who participated, qualifies as a war crime. Will charges be brought against NATO commanders? That will be the acid test of real justice.

Introduction

B-25s to B-29s

One windy day in the spring of 1942 the skies above Japan were filled suddenly with the sounds of strange aircraft that appeared out of nowhere. Sixteen twin-engine bombers with U.S. markings bombed Japan. The B-25 medium bombers of Lieutenant Colonel Jimmy Doolittle, launched from the USS *Enterprise,* were raiding Japan in retaliation for the December 7, 1941, attack on Pearl Harbor. The bombing did virtually no damage, but the shock to the Japanese people was enormous. They had been told that it was unthinkable that enemy aircraft would ever violate the skies over Yamato. But the unthinkable had happened.

Those living in Japanese cities asked the city governments what they were going to do about civil defense. Some recalled that the London underground transportation system had been used as an air-raid shelter during the Blitz. Could the Tokyo subway system be put to the same use?

No, said civil defense authorities. The Tokyo subway system was too shallow to give protection against high-explosive bombs. Civilians were told that they must build their own air-raid shelters. Newspapers began printing plans for simple shelters; civil defense authorities supplied buckets and flails and shovels and advised people to build cisterns on their property. The newspapers also announced plans to spray wooden houses with fire-retardant chemicals. But the chemicals were not available, so the houses went unsprayed. Civil defense authorities set up block programs involving all people, young and old. Each morning from 5 to 7 o'clock, training sessions were held in various districts.

New factories were built outside the cities, but the old factories remained. The new factories were constructed of steel and reinforced concrete; the old were built of wood, many in cities so crowded that housing districts were

1

intermingled with the factory sites. The Home Ministry informed company managers that they would be responsible for their employees. Company officials made plans to build air-raid shelters, and through neighborhood associations told their employees that they would have to dig their own shelters, either in their garden or under the house.

But for the large part, most of these plans were ignored, because the central government never admitted that it was possible for the enemy to raid Japan's cities. This was official government policy until the summer of 1944.

After the bombings in early 1942, Japanese Navy officers made plans to invade Midway Atoll and the Aleutian islands, from where they thought the U.S. bombers had come. Soon enough, the Japanese learned that the Doolittle raid had been launched from an aircraft carrier six hundred miles off the Japanese shore, but they were committed to the Aleutians invasion and carried it out. In fact, the Americans had considered using the Aleutian bases as a springboard for bombing Japan, but rejected the plan because the weather was so bad.

For a year Japanese and Americans battled in these northern wastes until the Japanese suddenly withdrew. During that year, engineers and technicians at the Boeing Aircraft Company in Seattle, Washington, developed the new superbomber, with which they proposed to carry out an air war against Japan. The development was closely followed by the Japanese high command through leaks in the international press.

When the new superbombers were ready in 1943, they were sent to India and western China. China, as it turned out, was too long a haul for the new superbombers, and the raids were confined to Manchuria and the tip of Kyushu, the most westerly of the Japanese home islands. They did remarkably little damage to the Japanese war effort.

The first B-29 raid on Japan was against Yawata Steel Works on Kyushu, which produced 27 percent of Japan's rolled steel. Seventy-five B-29s conducted that raid, coming in at high altitude (30,000 feet). Fifteen planes bombed visually, thirty-two bombed Yawata by radar, and the rest bombed other targets. It was not a very successful raid, but psychologically it was important. For the first time since Doolittle's raid, Japan had been bombed.

In December 1943, a Japanese military writer predicted that victory in the Pacific would come through air power. The Americans began searching for a new base for B-29 operations. Less than a year later, they found their new base, in the Mariana Islands.

The first B-29 mission was flown from Saipan in the Mariana Islands on November 24, 1944. Seventeen planes aborted but most of the planes bombed targets in Japan. Although it was difficult to see from 35,000 feet how much damage had been done, Washington claimed that "Tokyo's war industries have been badly hurt. No part of the Japanese Empire is now out of range." That statement was only too true. And Japan's air defenses were not equipped to combat this new threat.

Three days later the B-29s returned to Tokyo. The bombing was dreadfully inaccurate; the real damage was to the morale of Tokyo's citizens. Their worst fears were being realized.

At about this time Motoyuki Manabe had his first look at a B-29. He had been a soldier in the Imperial Army in Manchuria, but was discharged and had come to Tokyo to edit and write for *Shosen* magazine. He was standing on the street near the magazine office in Kanda one November day when he heard the air-raid sirens and, looking up, saw a large silver airplane high in the sky—so high it was leaving contrails behind it. So he had met B-san! It was a sight to remember.

Manabe continued to work for the magazine and experienced a number of air raids. It was hard to maintain his concentration on a manuscript with bombs falling all around, but he managed to do quite well. On November 24, 1944, he was reading galley proofs when the air-raid siren began to blow. He continued to read.

An old man from the accounting department was sitting across from him. "Air raid," the old man blurted out, and leaped out of his chair.

Manabe continued to read, neither moving nor changing his expression. It turned out, as it frequently did, to be a false alarm.

"When the air-raid siren blew, because you were supposed to leave your desk we always ended up getting behind in our work, and we could not meet regular publication deadlines," Manabe recalled.

"I became quite audacious. One day that month, for the first time in my life I witnessed an air battle. For five days we had been called out time and again by false air-raid alarms. A young girl in the office had her desk next to mine. This day she suddenly began to flutter around and went to the window and pressed her face to the glass.

"'Manabe san,' she called in an excited voice. 'Come quick! Come quick! B-29s—ten—twelve . . .'

"I went to the window and looked out," Manabe said. "Down in the street people were lined on both sides of the road, standing under the eaves of the buildings, looking up. The air-raid sirens were blowing. Japanese fighter planes were coming to attack the bombers. An air battle was about to begin.

"As we stood with our noses pressed against the glass, Japanese fighters attacked, and it seemed that they shot down a B-29; but we could not be sure, because the air fight passed out beyond our depth of vision.

"So it was all over. I went back to my desk and resumed reading proof," he said.

These air raids were remarkable because they began in 1944 as attacks on military targets, but in the spring of 1945 changed into an attempt to destroy the economic and social structures of Japan.

By 1944 the war was going badly for Japan. Early successes in 1941 and 1942 had brought a euphoria that was not justified. The Japanese people had begun to believe that their military forces were invincible. The Imperial Navy carefully concealed the major U.S. victory at the battle of Midway. The long battle for Guadalcanal and the ultimate Japanese defeat were minimized. As the U.S. military steadily made its way across the Pacific, the Japanese government claimed it was waiting for the right moment to strike back and destroy the U.S. fleet.

In reality, General H. H. Arnold, commander of the U.S. Army Air Forces, was committed to the strategic bombing of Japan that had been carried out more or less successfully by the British Royal Air Force and the Allies against Germany. So far the strategic bombing campaign in the Pacific had scarcely gotten off the ground.

By the end of 1944 the United States, with its air bases on Saipan, Tinian, and Guam, was ready to carry out a full-fledged bombing campaign against Japan. What was needed now was a tough, assertive, ruthless commander. He was found in the person of Major General Curtis LeMay, a professional Air Force officer who had earned his stars while serving in Europe with the 8th U.S. Army Air Force.

LeMay came in the middle of a great debate within the American military community, concerning the morality of bombing civilian populations. The debate had begun years earlier, when the Japanese began bombing civilian populations in China. The bombing of Shanghai had shocked the international community. Pictures of a Chinese child sitting, crying amid the rubble of the Shanghai railroad station, had appeared in newspapers throughout the world.

But since that time, the world had become hardened; in 1940 Germany set out to destroy London, Britain retaliated with raids on Berlin and other German cities, and the air war escalated. In 1943 the United States joined the battle and with the RAF the 8th U.S. Air Force destroyed Hamburg and Dresden by fire. One of the architects of this policy had been a young general: Curtis LeMay.

One of LeMay's early observations, after the city of Hankow, on the Yangtze River, was burned, was that Asian houses burned easily. This flammability was particularly true of Japanese houses, which were constructed largely of paper and wood.

The raids from the Marianas in late 1944 were conventional high-altitude raids. The bombers came in at 20,000 to 30,000 feet, bombed, and turned back for the Marianas. As late as March 4, 1945, 150 B-29s in four sections flew over Tokyo and bombed from high altitudes, knowing that the Japanese did not have antiaircraft guns that could reach above 25,000 feet and that Japanese fighter planes were not equipped for high-altitude interception. The bombers began at 8:30 in the morning. Their high explosive bombs did some damage, and their incendiaries started some fires. But in two hours the vigilant Tokyo firemen had extinguished the flames.

The American bombing strategy was about to undergo a radical change. On February 25, 1945, LeMay sent a bombing mission against Tokyo loaded with incendiaries. The weather was cloudy and the bombing was not assessed by photographs for several days. When the photos came in, they showed that one square mile of Tokyo had been almost obliterated. And this bombing had been done from high altitude.

What would happen if the same sort of bombing were done from low altitude?

To find out, General LeMay sent a training mission against Kito Io, a Japanese-held island in the Marianas. It was a small place with a jut of land that was very like one in Tokyo. The bombers were to go in at fifty feet above sea level to drop their bombs. The result: all the buildings on the island were obliterated.

After a few more failed high-altitude missions, LeMay switched to low-altitude incendiary missions against residential areas. He knew what this would do: change the focus of the bombing from military targets to civilian. No longer would the B-29s attack aircraft, tank, and engine factories. Now they would concentrate on burning up Japan.

On March 7, civilians in Tokyo and other Japanese cities braced themselves for another visit by B-san, the big silver bombers they had come to recognize. But only four B-29s appeared in Japanese skies that day; one bombed Okayama, and two bombed Shikoku. A fourth B-29 appeared over the Kanto plain, but did not drop any bombs. When the sirens wailed, the people took to their bomb shelters. Most families by this time had built private bomb shelters, usually nothing more than a pit covered for protection from splinters. But on this day in Tokyo no bombs were dropped.

On March 8, the Tokyo newspapers reported that B-29s had conducted reconnaissance flights over the area, nothing more. The average Japanese civilian was only dimly aware of the latest development regarding B-29s and the desperate fighting that was occurring on Iwo Jima. They didn't realize that the United States wanted Iwo Jima for an airfield to house fighters capable of escorting the B-29s to Tokyo and back.

The Japanese newspapers on March 9 were filled with stories about the heroic Japanese airmen who battled the B-29s. One of these heroes was Lieutenant Heikichi Yoshizawa.

> Lieutenant Yoshizawa, who shot down two B-29s and damaged several others in a series of B-29 raids on Tokyo, also damaged another B-29 when the enemy attacked the Kanto district. Although his plane was damaged by enemy gunfire, he deliberately launched a ramming attack on another enemy plane and downed it, thereby meeting a glorious death.

Then came March 9, 1945, and a revolutionary development in the air war over Japan.

General LeMay undertook to burn up the nation.

This book is the story of that horrifying campaign, in which the civilian population, rather than the military, became the target on the theory that parts for aircraft and other weapons were being manufactured in Japanese homes.

Some of the material in this book appeared in *The Night Tokyo Burned* (St. Martin's Press: New York, 1987). But the emphasis of that book was on the bombing. The emphasis of this book is on the bombing's effect on the people and government of Japan and the long-range effect this campaign had on warfare.

1

Firestorm

The high-altitude precision bombing campaign was not getting the job done in Japan. That much was apparent to General Curtis LeMay after the raid March 4, 1945, on the Musashimo Tama plant near Tokyo. Bad weather caused the bombers to miss their target, hitting instead the Tokyo urban area; this eighth raid on the Musashimo Tama plant left it virtually untouched.

But the February 25 raid on Tokyo, in which many of the bombs were incendiaries, was much more successful: 450 tons of firebombs had burned a square mile of Tokyo, destroying or damaging 28,000 buildings.

General LeMay called his wing commanders to meet at his Quonset hut headquarters on Guam. He showed them the results of the Tokyo firebomb raid and said he was encouraged: the Americans could burn the heart out of Japan's twenty largest cities, using M-69 firebomb clusters. His XXI Bomber Command was going to switch to night raids.

Moreover, they were going to change their entire tactics. No more high-altitude raids. They would go in low, five thousand to six thousand feet, and the crews would be reduced to save weight for more bombs. Anticipating objections, LeMay said that some of his flak experts believed such raids would be suicidal, but he disagreed. Japanese antiaircraft defenses were nothing like the German, LeMay knew from his European Theater experience. He anticipated losses due to flak would be only 5 percent. Seeing the quizzical looks on the faces of his audience, he went on.

Only two aircraft had been lost to flak to date because the Japanese relied on searchlights and radar, while the German flak batteries were controlled electronically. Initially, the low-level attackers would have the advantage of surprise in Japan.

What about fighters? somebody asked.

7

That would not be a problem. The Japanese had only two groups of night fighters in all the home islands, LeMay said. That's why I'm sending in the B-29s without machine guns or ammunition."

Major General Emmett "Rosie" O'Donnell, commander of the 73rd Wing, gave a low whistle. The others sat, stunned.

"Frankly," LeMay said, "I'm removing the ammunition because I'm afraid that the crews will be shooting at each other more than at the Japs. Then, too, we'll save three thousand pounds, which will give us another ton and a half of bombs."

That meant a 65 percent increase in bomb capacity.

He knew that the crews had not been trained for night missions but night missions it would be. "It is my hope," the general said, "that night missions will reduce losses at sea, because returning B-29s will be over Iwo in daylight." Iwo Jima had been captured, at great cost in Marine lives, a few months before, specifically to house emergency landing facilities for the B-29s.

General LeMay ended the meeting with a few remarks about the coming invasion of Okinawa. The B-29s would mount an all-out effort before that invasion, he said, beginning with a series of strikes on Japan's largest cities.

The first raid in the new program was announced a few hours later. It would be Tokyo, the Japanese capital and center of its war effort.

On March 9 plans were made for a succession of four raids—Tokyo first, and then on alternate nights Nagoya, Osaka, and Kobe. The first raid would take off in a few hours. The aircrews were summoned to a big galvanized steel hut with a barrel vault roof on Guam. They sat on long backless benches, pilots in the front row, the others behind. Intelligence officers handed out the briefing folders with the latest word from meteorologists. On the walls were maps, charts, and poop sheets assembled for the briefings. It was the same story on Saipan and Tinian.

The group commanders got up first and announced the mission's five points:

1. A series of night attacks will be made on major Japanese cities.
2. Bombing will be carried out from five thousand to eight thousand feet.
3. No armament or ammunition will be carried and the size of the crews will be reduced accordingly.
4. Aircraft will attack individually.
5. Tokyo will be the first target.

When the commander finished, the big room was filled with a silence so thick one could hear himself breathe. The fliers were in deep shock.

No guns; no ammunition; target Tokyo; attack at low altitude; individual attack.

The aircrews tried to digest what all this would mean: They would be sitting ducks for all the flak! The plans contradicted everything these fliers had been taught about attacking, including the need to keep tight formation for mutual protection. "Tojo loves stragglers" had been the old watchword.

But suddenly all had changed. Everybody was going to be a straggler!

The intelligence officers emphasized the purpose of the mission: to burn up a large section of Tokyo and thus damage Japan's ability to produce war materials. It would also hurt the Japanese civilian morale.

Individual attack would mean less time in the air, because aircraft would go directly from base to target, bomb, and then return to base. Attacking from different angles would lessen the danger of being tracked by the enemy and fired upon. (It would also increase the danger of air collision, but this was not mentioned.)

By reducing the size of the crew and abandoning guns and ammunition, bomb capacity could be increased by six to eight tons. By flying at lower altitude they would encounter better weather.

To raise morale, the intelligence officers told the men how important it was to destroy Japan's cottage aircraft industry. By burning up the big cities, they would burn out hundreds, and perhaps thousands of small home factories. After one intelligence officer had finished, another got up and described the routes to be taken on their 3,000-mile journey, the check points, assembly points, and aiming points. They were told what sort of bombs they would carry, the flak they might expect, the number and types of fighters they might encounter.

The meteorologists gave them the latest weather reports. The aircrews had suspected the weather would be lousy, because it was almost always lousy over Japan these days. But the meteorologists had a pleasant surprise for them this day: high winds were expected over the target, which meant their incendiaries would create fires that would spread quickly.

The briefing then broke up into specialist groups: aircraft commanders, navigators, engineers, radio operators. After, the fliers went back to their barracks, picked up their personal gear, went to the latrine, and then took a nap or stood around talking—or just stood around. They went to the mess halls for a meal, then piled into the trucks and began the dusty trip to the flight line. The closer mission time came the less talk there was. No one wanted to discuss how some of them would not come back.

The aircrews were not the only nervous ones this day. General LeMay had taken an enormous gamble with this decision to revolutionize the air war over Japan. His career was on the line: If he was wrong and the mission turned out to be a disaster, undoubtedly the XXI Bomber Command would have a new leader within a few days.

The tension on the U.S. airfields was high. For thirty-six hours the ground crews had been working to get the mission off the ground. The planes were still being worked over. Bombs were still being loaded from the dollies. Clusters of M-69 incendiaries were hoisted into the bomb bay by wire slings. When dropped from a plane, a time fuse would separate the clusters and individual six-pound bombs would spatter onto Japanese rooftops.

The aircrews stowed their Mae Wests, canteens, parachutes, oxygen masks, and perhaps a magazine or paperback book. Here and there a plane was scratched from the mission because it was inoperable or marginal.

The aircrews boarded. The radar operator sat down at his scope. The radioman sat at his table. Some men produced rabbits' feet or lucky dollars; some took out pictures of sweethearts or wives and put them where they could see them during the long flight ahead.

No guns, no gunners. What a change!

The captain started engines. They warmed for a while, revving and ebbing, then came the order: "Close bomb bay doors."

The flight engineer turned a switch and the four bomb bay doors swung closed in the belly of the Superfortress. "Doors and hatches closed," the flight engineer called.

Pilot and copilot closed the side windows of their compartment. The airplane was now sealed off from the world, a self-contained fighting unit ready for action. The noise level dropped and the smells changed; the dust and oil stink of the airfield was replaced by the metallic odors of an airplane as the B-29s began taxiing along the runway, lurching a little, like monsters out of their element.

Rain had fallen during the day and now at dusk the rays of the setting sun lighted up the tropical trees and shrubs, casting eerie shadows among the silver aircraft.

General LeMay stood on the north field at Guam, cigar clenched in his teeth, and watched the planes of the 314th Wing take off, his chief of staff, General August Kissner, by his side. As the last plane left the runway, LeMay turned and headed back for his headquarters to begin the long vigil, waiting for first reports.

The air armada was on its way, 324 Superfortresses carrying nearly two thousand tons of firebombs destined for Tokyo, 1,500 miles away. Out in front were the Pathfinders, who would provide the aiming points.

On that evening of March 9, the air defenses of the Kanto Plain were on the alert. Several night fighter units were in the Katsuura area, preparing for an air raid.

By 10 o'clock that night the winds had increased to sixty miles an hour and shortly afterward to eighty miles an hour. The high winds interfered with radio and radar reception, causing distortions and breaking down many antennae. Further difficulty was caused by the parallel systems of army and navy defense. At sea, navy picket boats were sending messages from as far away as a thousand miles. The messages were received by navy shore stations in Japan, but the army was not hooked into the navy system, so the night fighter squadrons on the Kanto Plain were not advised to get into the air.

A frantic call came at midnight from coast watchers on Fushan Island, reporting B-29 engines passing over the island. Eastern Army Command received this report at 12:30, and another from the station on Tsuki island that bombers were overhead. The army put out a call: "Major air raid on Tokyo."

What surprised the defenders was that the bombers were coming in low— the altitude was below 10,000 feet, not the 30,000 feet of the past.

It was soon apparent that the attack area would be the Koto basin between the Sumida and Ara rivers, an industrial district mixed with housing—twenty-five square kilometers. The pathfinders dropped their flares. General Thomas H. Power, commander of the 314th Wing, dropped his bombs first, then climbed to 10,000 feet and circled the city. Behind him Superfortresses from the three wings came in to bomb. Power watched as small fires erupted and then seemed to converge until huge areas were covered with flames. The surface winds increased and spread the flames. Fire leaped across the rivers and fire breaks as if they were not there. Two minutes later the bombers dropped in other spots and fires began to spread in the area inhabited by 400,000 people.

In fourteen minutes the inferno began.

The updrafts from the fires rocked Power's B-29, and he saw other bombers going straight up at a rate of two hundred or three hundred feet per minute.

There was very little antiaircraft fire from the ground, so complete was the surprise. A few fighters appeared but they did not attack, not knowing that the bombers were not carrying guns or ammunition. But within the hour the antiaircraft gunners recovered from their shock and began firing. Fighters moved in to attack when they found B-29s captured in the glare of the searchlights. In all, fourteen B-29s were shot down and forty-two were damaged. But air-sea rescue teams saved five of the fourteen crews.

On that terrible night of March 9, twelve-year-old Toshiko Higashikawa fought for her life against the firestorm. She was a sixth-year pupil at the Shinbari National People's School. She had spent eight months at the Miyagi Provincial School Evacuation Center and had returned to Tokyo to prepare for high school. On that night, when it became apparent that the bombers were really coming, Toshiko's mother sent the children into the family air-raid shelter in the garden.

Toshiko and the other children crouched in the darkness in their *monpei* and protective hoods. Their mother and father were above in a room packing the family belongings.

"We were telling each other everything was going to be all right," she recalled. "'Pull yourselves together,' I told the others."

In the sky above, the B-29s were dropping their firebombs and the blazes were spreading. The air was filled with fire and burning debris from flaming houses. People were running in the streets.

Toshiko continued her story: "'Damn!' Father said. 'It looks like we have got to leave here. We'll escape to the school. All right, get the children. Don't shilly-shally. Everyone! Quickly!'

"Mother brought us out of the shelter and into the house. Our belongings were piled on the floor. Father had put on his overcoat; Mother was all bundled up, ready to go.

"'Kazuyo,' she said, 'get Katsubo's cradle pack. Toshiko, get your rucksack.'

"I went upstairs to my room. My rucksack was lying by the futon and my clothes were there. I crammed them into the rucksack with an important textbook.

"'Toshiko,' Mother called from downstairs. 'Where ever have you got to?'

"'Wait a minute, Mama,' I replied.

"'Toshiko, what are you doing? We have to get going!'

"I grabbed my rucksack and ran down to join the others," Toshiko said. "As I ran in the light from the fires I noticed the wall calendar. It said March 9.

"We hurried through the streets, joining the fleeing crowd. Buildings were burning everywhere. Father was wearing his big backpack. It was very scary and the hot wind from the fires burned our faces. When a plane came over very low, we all ducked and tried to hide ourselves. We could see the bombs coming out of the planes; sometimes they exploded in the street in front of us. There was fire everywhere. I saw one person caught by the claws of the fire dragon before you could say Jack Robinson! Her clothes just went up in flames. Another two people were caught, and burned up. The bombers just kept coming.

"Father was carrying my little brother and had my sister by the hand. We came to the school. The tower of Hakko Ichiu near the school was on fire. Somehow we got separated at the public drinking fountain.

"A civil defense officer was shouting. 'No water here. If we stay here we will all be burned to death!' At the same time the fire was pouring out black smoke.

"'Oh,' I thought, 'We have all gotten separated!' We were jostled by waves of people. We walked and walked."

In the school's entryway waves of people, one after another, pushed and shoved. The public shoe box was on fire and spewing black smoke. No one could move, they were so tightly jammed in. Panic had developed and Toshiko could hear people shouting: "Gya. Help! It's hot! Mama! Uwa!" "Daddy! It hurts! Help!"

She heard her father shout: "Toshiko! Toshiko! Are you all right?"

"My hand fell off father's backpack," she recalled. "Father's face got lost in the crowd. Utako and I were drowning in the wave of people. Up above the fire was so bad you couldn't breathe. I don't know how long this went on. I felt faint. Over my head the shoe box was burning.

"To escape certain death I had to rely on myself. 'Older sister. Ne chan.' I heard Utako's voice but I could not see her.

"'Here! Here!' she said.

"'I can't crawl out of here. I am resigned, my eyes are closing,' I said.

"'Ne chan! Help! Help!' she cried.

"Fallen people's hoods and clothes are catching fire! *I will try one more time to crawl out of here,* I thought.

"'Ah! I have escaped! 'Utako! Utako!' I cry. Crawling through the smoke, I have gotten turned around. 'Ne Chan,' Utako called from under the mountain of bodies. 'I am over here!' I reached Utako. I rescued her.

"My eyes were sore and hurting from the smoke. So were hers. As we searched for the rest of the family, we were running as if in a dream. We could not find them, although Mother was not far away. Mother and Sister Kazuyo were talking. Sister Kazuyo said, 'Katsubo is dead because of me. I am finished' she said. 'Katsubo was screaming on my back when we were running away, but I couldn't do anything for him.' "

When Toshiko and Utako looked around, the town had turned into a burning wilderness. Nothing was left. Then Toshiko heard Mother's voice: "Hello. Do I hear Kazuyo's big sister's voice?" Toshiko was talking to Utako. Mother was talking to Kazuyo: "Kazuyo, you didn't kill Katsubo, don't feel guilty."

Then Toshiko saw them. "There's Mother," she shouted.

There in the safety of that forced evacuation center, mother and daughters met. It was a miracle! But from that day, Toshiko's father and brother Eichi were never seen again. Katsubo, who was just one year and seven months old, was dead. He had lived a very short life.

On that fateful night, thirteen-year-old Koji Kikushima was living in a house with six people in Kototoi Bashi. The fire had already spread to many houses on the opposite bank. The antiaircraft guns were firing—"Patsu patsu"—and lighting up the sky. The family took household goods and fled onto the Kototoi bridge. "We must not get separated," his father said in a loud voice.

Koji was in front with his bicycle loaded with household goods. Behind the bike, his mother and elder sister were pushing. A strong gust of wind caught the futon on fire. Everyone was pouring water on it.

Children were hanging onto their mother's coattails anxiously as the fire thrust at them. Koji recalled the sounds of the chaos: "Don't stop, ratatat tat. Keep moving. Look out! Don't push!" "Clear the way. Clear the way!" "The fire truck is stalled in the crowd!" "This fire engine is about burn up!" "Wa! Kyaaaaa!" People's bundles were catching fire, one after the other.

"Father was shouting," he said. "The hot wind of the fire moved around to attack everyone. I brushed sparks off my cheeks.

"Little sister Harue was shouting, 'Mother. It's hard to breathe!'

"'Harue, have patience!' Mother cried. Mother unfastened her fire hood, and covered Harue with it.

"People unable to stand the heat one by one climbed over the railing and jumped into the river. On the bridge one by one people's possessions burned.

"Father, I am going to lead the way," Koji recalled saying as he grasped Harue's hand and ran. "Harue! Come! Hurry!" They pierced their way into the crowd. The fire blast hit one side. They climbed over heads and luggage until they reached the balustrade. Then Koji led Harue over the balustrade and they jumped into the Sumida River.

The great fire burned on the bridge. On the far shore Sumida Park provided a fire line that ended up containing the fire.

When dawn came, Koji and Harue came out of the river and tried to retrace their steps. They searched for their parents, sister, and brother on the bridge, and asked others if they had seen them. The bridge, with its mountain of corpses, offered the only answer.

After the horror ended, and years after the war, time and again Koji dreamed about a mountain of bodies on the bridge. He never again saw his parents, his elder sister, and younger brother.

Sumiko Morikawa, a twenty-four-year-old homemaker living in Honjo's Higashi Komagata, was frightened by the daily air raids. She had a four-year-old son, Kiichi, and twin girls, Atsuko and Ryoko, eight months old. Her husband was in the army somewhere in Japan, waiting to go overseas.

On this night a neighbor helped Sumiko and her children flee from the fire to Yokogawa Park. Houses were burning and creating a vacuum, sparks and flames were dancing.

"Atsuko, Ryoko, have patience," she recalled telling her girls.

"Kiichi, don't hold onto Mother's hand," she told her son. "Mother will hold onto your hand and run."

As the fire closed in, they rushed to the park's pool. When they got there, Sumiko began ladling water out of the pool onto the children's backs. Other people began clustering at the pool. The fire was blowing in a vortex and flames were shooting through.

A sudden gust of fiery wind blew sparks at Sumiko. Kiichi was crying. "Okachan, okachan, It's hot!" Kiichi's air-raid hood and jacket were on fire. As Sumiko doused the flames, she saw the red flames reflected in the water. She had to save her children. First, she got into the pool with the babies on her back. Then she pulled her son into the pool and doused him with water.

The fire was closing in. The Yokogawa National People's School buildings were burning and bright red flames gushed out of the windows. People were jumping into the pool. Soon there was no room around the pool.

A fireball struck Kiichi in the head. Like an insane person Sumiko was ladling water on the children. "Mother, it's hot!" Kiichi said.

"Hang on hang on. Don't go to sleep. We can see Father very soon," she told him. She tapped on his cheek desperately. But Kiichi opened his eyes listlessly and then slumped over. In the meantime, the twins had died.

"Kiichi, Kiichi, don't leave me alone," she said.

Sumiko fainted. When she came to and looked around, the water in the pool had dried up. Kiichi was still breathing very faintly and shivering. She took him in her arms and walked up onto the side of the pool. She asked forgiveness from her two daughters.

"We have a rescue station over there," a civil defense officer told Sumiko as he pointed. "You hurry along and take your son to the doctor. But you must leave your two daughters because they are dead. There is a rule, you cannot move the bodies of the dead even if they are your family."

Once again Sumiko apologized to her twin daughters and covered them with her wet jacket. She could not stop crying.

She took Kiichi on her back to the rescue station, but there was no doctor there. She managed to take her son to a friend's house, where there were many, many refugees. She wrapped Kiichi in a futon and held him. A girl gave her a cup of hot tea. She filled her mouth with tea and then, like a mother bird, she transferred the tea to Kiichi's mouth. He opened his eyes a little, said "Mama," and then he slumped over again, dead.

Years later, Sumiko still felt responsible for the deaths of her three children on that horrible night.

Soldier Motoyuki Manabe had moved out of the center of Tokyo to Setagaya, and so he was outside the action zone this night. But a friend was in the middle of it. Her name was Toshiko Tsurumaki and she was a third-year student at a girls' high school in Asakusa district. Under the mobilization laws, even junior high school students were drafted. Toshiko's war work was at the Tokyo Electric Train Company in Mukojima, where she made gun cartridges. The work was exhausting, and if she got tired, that was just too bad. There was a war on.

The night of March 9, a tired Toshiko had climbed into her futon and pulled the covers up. The air-raid warnings had gone off at 10:30. The radio warned that a single aircraft was sighted in the Boso area, heading for the home islands. But Toshiko was so tired and the cotton felt so good that she did not budge. Besides, a few B-29s, coming in one by one, were nothing to worry about. Sure enough, that's how it turned out. The next report said the enemy planes were fleeing south. There was no problem. She fell into a sound sleep.

"Toshiko, Toshiko! Air raid. Get up." Her elder sister called her. It was time to go to the Mukojima factory. Elder sister was up that night because she was nursing her husband, Chuuji Kusaka, who was manager of a sake distillery. He was sick and growing worse.

Toshiko didn't want to get up; she didn't want to go to the factory. It was so nice in bed. She complained bitterly. "Tell them I'm not coming."

"Get up," her sister called. "Hurry up."

There was no way to avoid it. Finally Toshiko got up from the futon. She got ready as she usually did, put on a rucksack, nimbly fastened it and was off. She was just thinking the fire department air-raid shelter outside would ward off danger when she heard the call. "People outside please come into the air-raid shelter. Because there is danger, hurry up. Please."

Zu . . . zun, bang! Something dreadful—the sound of an explosion could be heard. Thirty seconds later something struck: a direct hit from a firebomb!

A pillar of fire rose up outside. As might be expected, Toshiko was startled. She sprang from the shelter, like one in a dream, and rushed into the main street. Her sister and brother-in-law followed. What they saw amazed them.

The street was alive with fire. Down the street at a rate of more than twenty meters per second, a firestorm was blowing. The bombing attack had kindled many large fires, which the winds had whipped into a real firestorm. That firestorm was blowing in gusts.

In the middle of the street stood a handcart loaded with luggage and household goods. Toshiko's eyes swept the scene. There was a handcart, but it was deserted; no one was near it. The firebombs and firestorm had defeated whoever had been pushing the cart.

The wind blew in gusts like a living thing, Toshiko remembered. One person was running. Suddenly the fire connected with the luggage on the handcart; the fire reached out and grabbed the runner before Toshiko's eyes, and dragged her down. Hellfire was the word for it, she thought. Left and right, the street was becoming an ocean of flame.

That night's air raid was different from ordinary military operations, Toshiko recalled. She had heard on the radio at 10:30 that a single B-29 was spotted invading the Boso area. Shortly afterward it headed south. Naturally Tokyo people took off their fire hoods and put their futons out. The sirens sounded again two hours later and the air raid came. This time, firebombs fell like rain.

That first report of a single B-29 was obviously a decoy, causing the people to relax while the vast armada of enemy aircraft—about three hundred B-29s—followed. That night's military operation was a trick—a waiting game. Tokyo people were flurried by the attack.

General LeMay's plan was carried out by 298 B-29s. A single plane—a Pathfinder—skirted the ocean area at low altitude. That plane carried napalm M-47 bombs, which it dropped at thirty-meter intervals. The B-29s used this clear marker to drop M-69 firebombs at fifteen-meter intervals. After dropping the firebombs, the planes pursued a course to Tokyo Bay and Edo Gawa Ward, Koto Ward, Chuo Ward, Minato Ward, Oota Ward, north to Katsushika Ward, Kita Ward, Itabashi Ward, west to Shinjuku Ward, as far as Shibuya Ward. This area is called Kawamuko, which means Shitamachi—Lower City. That area and part of Yamanote were included. The attackers uniformly scattered firebombs throughout the area.

Flying at five hundred kilometers per hour, the B-29s scattered the bombs in less than an hour. Because of the shortage of Japanese fighter planes and antiaircraft guns, the B-29s' operations went unchallenged. In the twinkling of an eye this entire area was rolled up and finished.

The M-69 firebombs were scattered among the houses, producing many unusually big, strong fires, what the Japanese firefighters called *goryu kasai* (linked fires). Forty percent of Tokyo's houses (twenty-nine out of thirty-five wards) were affected. Fire engines had no chance against these fires; bucket brigades and such were not much more effective. People have since decided there was no "best way" to fight these fires.

The people fled before the wild fires with all their might. With strength born of desperation they forced their way through the crowds. However, the first ones found themselves up against another thick wall of fire. Then they fought their way through to the water barrels and doused themselves from head to toe. But their clothes dried quickly, and like withered leaves they caught fire in an instant, and blazed up.

When the rucksacks of running people caught fire, those behind them began to shout: "Hey, you, your fire hood is on fire!"

That was how it went.

People were fleeing the firestorm so as not to be roasted alive. The asphalt on the roads caught fire or dissolved, and roads turned into mud. Toshiko Tsurumaki stumbled over dead bodies rolling over and over. A young mother was lying face down on the road, her baby carried under her belly, thus protecting the baby with her posture. But the baby was already dead. The dead mother's hair was on fire.

A large group of refugees ran along the side of the road, but because of the corpses Toshiko couldn't see where they were going. And she had no time to spare. As she passed the dead young mother, she saw that the face was blackened by the fire; the woman had been burned to a crisp. This was a burning hell!

Toshiko brushed off the mud that covered her and ran on along the hot asphalt road, being careful not to burn her feet. Her elder sister was helping her sick husband. They were holding hands. Voices were asking what was going on . . . Running, running, running.

Toshiko heard a horrible noise, a buzzing. It was the propeller sound of a B-29 flying low through the red blizzard, soot falling all around.

The telephone poles appeared to dance as they burned. One telephone pole stood in front of the eaves of a house. It began to burn from the top, but it did not fall down. Then the next pole on the line began to burn. The hot wind began to blow in a little tornado that was spinning fast. It picked up the top part of the telephone pole and sent it curling up through the air.

To Toshiko it looked like a red blizzard, and in the soot of the fire the broken telephone pole danced. Burning in midair, the telephone pole danced faster and faster. Mattresses were also dancing, waiting to join the lump of fire, swimming in the sky.

The wind velocity reached twenty meters per second. Toshiko was almost falling down because of the strong wind, and she couldn't get her breath. She must have patience, she told herself as she ran from the whirlwind.

She ran five hundred meters south of Kikuya Bashi's main street to the crossroad, where on the left-hand corner stood the National People's School. The fire had already visited this place. The refugee crowd, like an avalanche, had arrived to die inside.

In greater Tokyo old people and children had already been sent to the countryside; primary–school-aged children had been evacuated in groups. Buildings were torn down to make a big space for other evacuees.

This building wasn't the greatest place for refuge. The school and the remaining government buildings had all been destroyed in the air raid, leaving plenty of open space, so Toshiko and her relatives made this place their goal.

The school was narrow inside and the school gate was gone, as were the glass doors on the facing road. Inside the concrete had become a dirt floor. On the left and right walls the *geta* boxes were gone, burned. Opposite the remains of the school garden were still there.

Toshiko pushed people's trash out of the way and water barrels to the side. One of the fire brigade people gave her a wet linen bag from an air-raid defense hood to protect her from the fire in the air. She put on the wet linen bag and lay on her face on the concrete floor. She lost consciousness. However, she instinctively put her hand over her mouth, as she had been taught during fire drills at elementary school.

When she recovered a short time later, the linen bag was gone—dropped or carried away. She didn't care about the linen bag. When Toshiko had first gone inside with the crazy crowd she hadn't seen her sister and her sister's husband. She wondered where they had gone. When she stood up, she saw a great number of people collapsed on the floor, motionless, as if dead. Truly, they looked dead, or exhausted. Either way, they did not move. (At that time many people were dying from smoke inhalation.)

Toshiko thought, "I don't want to die in this hell." She walked along the dirt floor of the school garden path. She felt very lonely. If elder sister died what would become of Toshiko? That would be unbearable, Toshiko thought. A painful feeling came over her.

The early morning before dawn was clear and cold, without a cloud in the sky. When the firestorm had passed earlier, the wind was like a knife. Now the temperature was dropping. It seemed that the cold wind was cutting into Toshiko's body as she searched for her elder sister.

The victims were overflowing the open space. She paused to listen at the sound of a voice. It was a small voice, very faint. "Toshiko, Toshiko." It was her sister's voice. Her sister was over there.

It looked as if the fire had caressed her sister's face and hands, causing them to swell. Her eyes were swollen and inflamed, just like Toshiko's.

Toshiko's sister had been buffeted about in the avalanche of people who descended on the school's front door. While she tended to her sick husband, she became separated from Toshiko.

As the sick husband was tossed about by the crowd, he realized his limitations. "Now I am going to die," he told his wife. "If you have to take care of me, you will not be saved. Go away and leave me alone, I am okay." He said it over and over again.

Still, Toshiko's sister had encouraged her husband. They went to the front door but there was no room to move because of the crowd. Then they retraced their steps, to the open space. The wind turned chilly as they waited for the night to end.

From far away they could hear the flow of voices of the volunteer squad members. "From the town offices we are distributing hard crackers. Please come," they said. They also distributed boiled rice, food, bedding and other supplies, and took care of the wounded. This was not the first time that they had handed out supplies.

At about noon Toshiko wanted to get some hardtack but didn't, because when she saw many airplanes flying low, she knew that she and the others were the targets. If she showed up in the open space, she feared she would be killed by the machine guns. So she sat still behind the sandbag barrier, holding her breath.

It was too bad. She sat there with her belly empty.

"Even though we suffered we were very lucky," her sister told her. "I heard that those who ran to Umaya Bridge were all killed."

"Umaya Bridge?"

"Yes," her sister said. "Last night we hesitated, deciding whether to go to Umaya or come here. It was good that we came here."

Her sister continued: "The crowd was going to the bridge. If we went to Umaya, we could not cross the bridge. From behind the fire was driving so it was hard to breathe. A large number of people fell into the river and appeared to die."

In this kind of turmoil even rumor seemed to spread like the wind. Elder sister heard many rumors: Asakusa's Kannon Temple of Mercy was burned down. On one bank of the Sumida River an ocean of fire had developed.

Later on, Toshiko realized that the stories her sister had told her were not rumors; they were facts. Later on, Toshiko, her sister, and her brother-in-law made their way to Fukushima Province in the north, opposite Hokkaido. This area was sparsely populated and quite primitive. There was no gas and they were forced to cook on a wood-burning stove.

Toshiko did not know how to use firewood, or how to cut kindling. Furthermore, she was terrified of fire. The first time her brother-in-law started the stove, she saw the flames and began to shake all over. Elder sister comforted her. "You will soon get over this fear," she said.

But Toshiko never did get over it. Even thirty years later, whenever she saw an open flame, her body went into uncontrollable spasms.

In Tokyo the damage caused by the firestorm of March 9 was tremendous on the Sumida River's two banks, Taito Ward, Sumida, Kooto . . . A great number of people drowned by the Umaya Bridge as they dodged the devastating fire below. The approach to the bridge, as far as they could see, was crowded with people pushing and pushing behind them. The fire's vortex whirled but they could not turn back. As a last resort they jumped into the river and drowned. It was indeed a Hobson's choice: Were they to be killed by the fire or drowned by the water? Either way, they would die.

The area near the Kototoi Bridge was more dangerous than the Umaya Bridge. That night in the Asakusa region the B-29s attacked in waves four times, setting three raging fires. Moreover, the fire in Asakusa assumed a triangular pattern that was impossible to control.

People fled, bewildered, in three directions, most carrying their luggage on their shoulders. Some sought refuge in Sumida Park, by the Sumida River. Before long, however, the fire climbed to Sumida Park, so many people headed upstream to Kototoi Bridge, crossing the bridge opposite Mukojima Island. The horrible fire even burned up most of Mukojima.

Countless refugees were heading in Asakusa's direction, crossing slippery roads. On both sides of the bridge they were struck from the rear by increasing numbers of people, and on the bridge, people could not move. A large dray wagon and several bicycle carts were jammed up. The congestion grew—pushing, pushing, trampling people, total confusion in the middle—bodies came to the surface of the mob, hands stuck up, and the mass overflowed so that some fell into the river.

If Kototoi Bridge had been made of wood, the girders would have broken because of the weight of all the people. But the steel girders did twist, adding more grief to the situation. The steel grew white-hot and people who touched the metal were seared like steaks on a barbecue.

The bridge was filled with innumerable people and their possessions. Embers and soot fell left and right, and piece by piece destroyed the baggage. That was the detonator. The air was overheated and the wind's speed was twenty meters per second. There was no escaping the dreadful heat. Luggage and people caught fire at the same moment; in a fraction of a second, the bridge was surrounded by a white corona.

Heat rays spread on the bridge, hitting and searing the running; many thousands of bodies were turned into black lumps of charcoal—objects no longer human.

The names, addresses, ages, even the genders of the charcoal bodies were unknown. The bodies were so twisted that when an army unit arrived, they could not count them—could not even separate them. When the tide changed, the blackened bodies piled up on the riverbank like cordwood; they even looked like burned logs. The soldiers came in big trucks to take the corpses away, using shovels to move the bodies and body parts into the trucks.

As they were loading the bodies, one soldier said: "About these bodies . . ."

Another soldier muttered: "About these bodies, what crime did they commit? In spite of their innocence, what sort of cook roasted them to death? War costs lives, but . . . Why this?"

Nineteen-year-old Kimie Ono lived with her parents in the Hamacho section of Nihonbashi district. Because of the damage to other family houses from earlier raids, on March 9 eight people were living in her house.

Kimie had gone to bed early and was sound asleep when the air-raid siren suddenly began to scream. She listened for a moment—the sound of the bombers was very loud. They must be very low over the city. That was unusual.

She had a premonition of disaster; she went to the front door and looked into the street. It was alive with fire, with houses burning on both sides. It was the middle of the night but the fires lit up the area as bright as noon.

She listened. The house was silent, empty. Everyone had gone. If she was to escape she would have to get going. She went to the kitchen and put some food in a rucksack and came back for another look. It was time to go. She opened the door, felt a blast of heat, stepped into the street, and headed toward Ryogokubashi, following the railroad line.

The street and railroad line were crowded, jammed with people trying to escape the inferno: mothers carrying babies, fathers with toddlers on their shoulders, old men with sleeping mats, grannies with pushcarts filled with household goods, a mass of people crowding, pushing, shouldering their way forward, hurrying to escape the flames behind them. The heat grew hotter, and people began to collapse on the roadside and in the road itself. More people came along and trampled them. They rushed toward the rivers.

The confusion was compounded by the fire winds, which scoured lanes among the people, separating families irretrievably. The searing winds at ground level were fifty miles an hour, and carried sparks and burning objects. Carts were abandoned along the way, but people staggered on, wave after wave of them. No one stopped to loot the fallen; to stop was to die.

The horror grew worse. A mother and child were ahead of Kimie, running. The firestorm swept out a tendril. And in a second, as she watched, mother and child were aflame, burning to death as they ran. They fell to the ground.

No one stopped to help them. Kimie shivered but she ran by, knowing that she should stop. But how could she? She was swept along in the mass of people, running, running, running from the flames.

Kimie passed a temple rice field. It was aflame, the rice crackling in the wind. She saw nine bodies crumpled in the field as she ran on and on. She came to the Hisamatsu Police Station.

"Can I go to the Akira shrine to find protection?" she asked.

"Impossible," the police officer replied. "The shrine is burned down."

In the crowd around the police station Kimie met her eldest sister. "What shall we do?" she asked.

"The river, the Sumida," she said. "We must get to the river and jump in. The water will protect us."

They ran on. But as they reached the bank of the Sumida, they saw bodies, the corpses of the burning who had sought the water for safety, bodies horribly burned and drowned. Dozens of them—floating downstream. Even as they watched, others came and jumped, some of them on fire.

"We must go back," Kimie said. She and her sister turned and retraced their steps, moving against the tide of people. But the firestorm had passed them by. They went by the temple rice field. It was blackened and smoking, but the fires were low. The firestorm had moved on to Yokoyama-cho.

Kimie Ono looked down at her *monpei*. They were badly burned. She looked back at the police station. It was old and very small. The Meiji Theater was very close, so they went there.

The Meiji Theater was one of Tokyo's landmarks, rebuilt in 1928. It was a modern building, four stories high, and with basement. It was designed after the great Tokyo earthquake and fire of 1923 to be earthquake- and fire-proof, and could seat more than 1,200 people.

Kimie and her sister went to the Meiji Theater and tried to get in. A man at the entrance told them to go anywhere else because it was so crowded. They had nowhere else to go so they begged to be allowed to stay. The man let them in.

Inside, they heard horrible noises from the basement, and Kimie felt that the place was just hell. In the meantime, the shutter of the building's entrance closed automatically. The people were trapped inside without any way to escape. She and her sister held hands and wondered what to do. Their parents were living in Hayama. Her sister's children were in Meguro. The family was completely safe. Her sister said to Kimie: "Kimi-chan, you can pretend I am your mother."

"If we are going to be killed by the fire, sister," Kimie said, "I will feel as if I were killed in my mother's arms."

Then Kimie and her sister hugged each other and cried.

The theater's dressing rooms were burning. The smoke was so thick they couldn't see any faces. Kimie put her kerchief over her nose and mouth to breathe. But her effort was in vain. Searching for a place to hide, and holding hands, the sisters climbed down into the basement. As they went, they heard a ghostly voice crying out in pain. Someone was dying.

When they got into the basement they saw a terrible sight: the person who was dying was someone they knew, a girl named Hayama, about the same age as Kimie's sister. They had visited the Hayama house many times. The two families were so close that their mother called the girl *kimichan*—baby. As they came up to Hayama-san and hugged her, she died. Kimie and her sister began to cry.

It was even hotter in the basement than it had been on the ground floor. Greasy sweat soon covered Kimie's entire body. At last she fainted in the smoke.

The Meiji Theater, that modern ferro-concrete building, was burning from the outside and inside, very rapidly. Scores of people were roasted to cinders, steamed to death, or suffocated. People were scraping at the walls with their fingernails, trying to get out. Months later one of Kimie's friends visited the Meiji Theater ruins and saw many traces of fingernails on the basement walls.

Suddenly, perhaps because of the intense heat, the automatic shutter opened. The crowd broke and dozens of people rushed outside. Kimie was lying unconscious near the entrance and they trampled her. She had a double dream: in one she happily chatted with her parents, but superimposed on that was the reality of being trampled by bare feet, shoes, and *geta*.

Kimie's feet began to feel like they were burning, and then she woke up. She saw the burning theater and a mountain of dead bodies, and realized she wasn't dreaming.

She knew that if she stayed there she would die. She grasped the knob of the door and tried to pull herself up but she could not walk. Summoning all her strength she managed to crawl to the underground shelter in front of the Meiji Theater. The shelter had no roof. It was full of people and when she appeared someone asked, "Where did you spring from?" Then she was grasped by friendly hands, which massaged her aching body.

At dawn the civil defense workers came to the shelter and called for the people to come out. In the early morning light Kimie saw that all the buildings had burned down but the Meiji Theater, which was still burning. She could hear bodies sizzling inside.

She had a sudden chill, as though someone had poured ice water over her body. Her body began to tremble uncontrollably. She looked around her.

Bodies were lying everywhere, some of them in kimonos. The scene resembled a ghastly tailor's window. People coming from the shelter were black, black and dirty, many of them wounded, all of them ragged, their *monpei* torn and filthy—pitiable sights.

She looked for water but there was none, only mud . . .

Miwa Koshiba was a young Tokyo homemaker who lived in Asakusa, near the temple. She and her husband had already sent three of their five children to stay with relatives in Gifu, near Nagoya. She had decided to keep the baby and their four-year-old daughter with them, because they were too young for school. Her six-year-old son was about to start elementary school and Miwa wanted to make him some new clothes, so her husband went to Gifu early in March and brought the boy back. On March 9, Miwa's mother Yae was sick in bed in the Asakusa house, and her father Ichibei was there, too. The family had always kept servants but now there were none. Miwa was wife, mother, cook, and nurse—all in one.

When the air-raid siren began the night of March 9, the family knew they would have to act swiftly. The only way to get the mother and father to a safe place was for her husband to carry her mother on his back and Miwa to lead her father to the nearby school, which was the "safe place."

But to do this, first the children had to be put in the family air-raid shelter, the hole they had dug in the garden. So the children were put in the shelter, the roof was fastened on, and then Miwa and her husband set out for the school with her mother and father. Then the husband stayed with the old people while Miwa went back to the house for the children,

By the time she had arrived home, the house was gone. The firestorm had eaten it, leaving only ashes. She rushed into the garden. The wooden cover to the air-raid shelter was on fire. She grabbed a bucket and went to the cistern they had installed for emergencies and began dousing the shelter cover with water. She put out the fire, tore away the cover, and, burning herself through the *monpei*, found her children inside. They were frightened and disheveled, but alive. Aiyawa, the six-year-old boy, was burned about the face and neck.

Miwa began to walk to the Sumida River, half a mile away. She carried the baby and urged the four-year-old and six-year-old to walk with her. The firestorm was still raging and they were moving along with it until they finally came to the bank of the Sumida. She found the bank ablaze, with people dropping all around her. She looked for shelter, and finally found a sewer pipe that emptied into the river. Without hesitating, she pushed the two children into the sewer and followed with the baby. The place stank of offal and it was hot, but there was no fire. She began to bathe the children with sewer water, to cool them off.

Miwa sat in the stinking sewer pipe all night long, bathing her children's faces to keep them cool. Three times the baby stopped breathing, but each time Miwa brought her back to life. How she did this she never knew because by the time she and the children had reached the sewer, Miwa's eyes were swollen shut and she could not see. They emerged from the filthy sewer in the morning and headed for the Fukagawa Middle School, where Miwa's husband, her mother, and her father had found safety.

Hiratsuka Saki lived in that area near the Sumida River through which Miwa Koshiba had struggled. On the evening of March 9, he noticed that the wind was blowing very hard, shaking the trees in the garden. At about 10:30 the siren began to wail. Then it stopped. There was to be no raid that night, it seemed.

Hiratsuka had been ready for bed, but the siren had awakened him, so he decided to stay up for a while. Then the siren began again just after midnight. Everybody was up, and Hiratsuka's mother decided they would go to the disaster shelter area nearby, as they had been told to do by the block warden. Hiratsuka and his father stayed behind to collect some bedding and food, filled two rucksacks, and then started out to join the women. As they left the house, Hiratsuka looked up and saw that the roof was on fire. He looked up the street; all the houses in his block were ablaze and the fire was lashing out across the street, driven by the high wind. The street that led to the shelter was an impassable wall of flame. He could feel the heat of the fire that was only fifty meters away.

Hiratsuka looked at his own house; it was now totally engulfed in flames. There was no safety to be found there. He and his father saw people hurrying into a concrete building—the Yasuda Bank—a few doors from his house. They dropped their rucksacks and the bedding and headed for the building.

Inside, the ground floor was crowded with people and their belongings, so the Sakis went to the basement. Other people crowded in, and soon there were about sixty in the basement. In the milling crowd Hiratsuka lost touch with his father. Half an hour later the shutters of the ground floor windows began to burn. The people in the basement moved away from the walls, which had grown hot. Hiratsuka found a valve in a pipe and turned it. Water came gushing out. He put his head under the valve and splashed water on himself. Around him, people began to collapse from the heat. In an hour, half of them were dead.

The water kept rising in the basement and the heat was ferocious. Saki felt his strength ebbing. Around him people were drowning in the hot water. Of the sixty people who had taken refuge here only Saki, his father, and four others were still alive.

The water level continued to rise, and the ceiling of the basement was pressing down on them. Bodies floated to the surface. They decided that Saki had to try to break out of the basement, so he climbed up to the door. It was very hot. He summoned all his strength and made an enormous lunge at the door. He could feel the searing of the metal on his hands but the door did not budge. He had failed. Death seemed inevitable.

But just then the door crashed open, battered from the outside by civil guards with sledgehammers.

Masatake Obata was one of those people General LeMay was talking about when he rationalized the firebombing campaign against Japan—a small manufacturer of airplane parts. He farmed out individual items to workmen in the area, assembled the components, and delivered the parts to another manufacturer.

Obata was a retired soldier. Long before, he had served his compulsory two years, then gone into the army reserves. He had kept up his reserve status though he had not expected to be called to active service again. He was too valuable as a manufacturer.

On March 9 there were eight people in the Obata household: Masatake, his wife, four children, and two sisters. His sisters lived in the Ueno district, near the big park, but were visiting the Obatas that afternoon. What with gossiping and drinking tea, they had stayed late, and when darkness fell, Obata had naturally asked them to stay overnight.

They had all heard the sounds of the first air-raid alarm and then the quiet that indicated nothing was to happen. When the alarm sounded again, Obata went outside and saw that it was the real thing. He hurried back into the house, changed into his air-raid warden's uniform and prepared to go on patrol.

He told his wife and children and the two sisters to get dressed, and then took them to Fuji Park, the designated safe area, where a crowd was assembling. He then hurried to a neighborhood association meeting. There he got new instructions that sent him back to Fuji Park, where he informed his relatives that they were to go to the larger Sumida Park.

Then Warden Obata went on patrol, in uniform with the conical steel helmet that was designed to protect his head from shrapnel. He moved from door to door in his neighborhood, checking each house to see that no one had been left behind. This air raid was something new, and the character of Japanese houses told him there was going to be a great deal of trouble this night. Obata found a number of people still in their houses, mothers tending babies, and older men and women. He told the people that they had to go to Sumida Park.

He waited until they complied, then moved on. In an hour he had finished his work, and he went into the main street again, heading for Sumida Park to meet his wife and children.

On the way he encountered many people who were complaining of the intense heat and the smoke that was making it hard to breathe. Most of the people had air-raid hoods but these did not offer much safety. He saw half a dozen people snatch the burning hoods off their heads. He saw one woman with her hair on fire. There was nothing Obata could do to help them. His own hood caught fire, and he began slapping at the flames.

Overhead the B-29s continued their deadly assault. Suddenly a cluster of six-pound incendiary bombs hit the ground ten feet away. Before Obata could move, one incendiary bomb tore loose from the cluster and was flung at him, exploding in his face. The helmet that was supposed to protect him funneled the force of the explosion directly against his jaw. The force of the explosion knocked him down and the steel helmet crashed against the hard roadbed. Warden Obata fell unconscious.

He awoke, not knowing how long he had been out. His feet hurt, and he looked at them. His shoes had burned up and his toes had melted. His arms and hands hurt; they were burned black and he knew he had third-degree burns. His clothing was still burning in spots. He could not use his hands, and so he rolled over and over to put out the flames. He managed to get to his feet and began to walk, heading for a trench on the side of the road. He knew that trench: he had helped dig it to protect tram riders of they were caught in an air raid.

Walking was difficult, for his feet had swelled up to three times their size; he felt as if he was walking on tennis balls. He finally made it to the trench, where he found seven other people, all suffering from serious burns. None of them knew how badly they were hurt but they could see how badly the others were hurt. One complained about being sleepy.

"Yes, and if you go to sleep you will die," Obata said. "You must stay awake, we must all stay awake or we are dead."

He told them that if they saw their neighbor dozing off to wake him. Then he led them in chanting. They chanted Buddhist prayers and pushed and punched each other to stay awake while they waited for dawn.

Masuko Harino worked in a factory and lived in a workers' hostel in Nihonbashi with many other young women. Every day the women would get up, eat breakfast, and go to Shinagawa to work in the Fukashi electric machinery factory.

When the firebombs began falling on the night of March 9, the fires threatened the hostel. "We will fight the fires to the last," the hostel manager said. Then he disappeared and was not seen again. The fires grew worse and soon engulfed the main building.

"As the worry grew over the fate of the hostel," Masuko, recalled, "one of the young people, Yoshikawa-san, and I went toward the factory. We were all fleeing together but somehow we two got separated from the others." When they had left the hostel, there were some seventeen or eighteen of the women.

"People's clothes were on fire, it had become a fiery drama," she said. "Some people were writhing in torment, but no one had time to help them.

"In front of me I saw the Meiji Theater. It was full of people, so many that we could not get inside. Intense heat was coming from the firestorm. My eyes seemed about to pop out of my head. Yoshikawa-san cut her way through the mob, and I followed her along the road, seeking some respite from the heat of the terrible fire. As we ran we saw fleeing shapes, but nothing else. A telephone pole collapsed, and twisted electric wires snaked out along the ground. The road on both sides was full of people's possessions, all of them burning up.

"My eyes hurt. It was hard to breathe and I thought I was dying. I found a hydrant that was working and soaked my *zukin* (air-raid hood) and put it back on, almost unconsciously. Finally I found I had fled as far as Kiyosu Bridge."

When she went to cross the Sumida on that bridge, the fire was bouncing like volleyballs. Looking toward the Honjo and Fukagawa districts she saw nothing but walls of flame. Her eyes smarted and soon hurt so badly she could not open them. She dropped down by the side of the road and found a *zabuton* (floor cushion). She wiped her hands and face with it, and found that it eased the pain.

People were leaping into the Sumida River to save themselves. She heard their voices but she could not make out what they were saying. All around her lay unconscious bodies covered with ashes. She lay there beside the road, all through the long night, waiting for the dawn.

Chiyoko Sakamoto, eight months pregnant, also lived in the Fukagawa district. She and her husband heard the air-raid siren and rushed out of their house with their child, but were stopped by the civil guards. They had started for the Sumida River, but as the guards pointed out to them, the flames there were shooting up, the wild flames of the firestorm.

They turned back but the firestorm came at them, and soon Chiyoko's eyes were closed from the grit and heat. She could scarcely think. She clutched at her husband. "*Ikemasen.* I cannot go on," she said. "I cannot go on." But her husband encouraged her to keep moving and as in a dream she fled the flames.

Even with her advanced pregnancy, they managed to stagger through the mounds of baggage and other people's burning possessions, toward the Sasaki red-light district, where they hoped to find refuge. They were pulled up by a police officer who told them the whole geisha district was burning and was impossible to enter. They could see the flames shooting up. (That night the entire geisha district burned. Sasaki, as well as Asakusa and the Tokyo area, lost its most famous geishas.)

Chiyoko and her husband moved along the Jukan River, traveling east. They saw atrocious sights: people with skin hanging down from their arms; people overcome by their burns, writhing in pain, screaming, with no one to help them in their terror and their torture. It was a world gone mad.

The Sakamotos came to a high wall surrounding the Chiba bus company. It seemed they would die if the fire dragon continued to come their way. And the fire dragon was coming. Chiyoko lost confidence and was preparing to die. But her husband grasped her hand just before the smoke and fire engulfed them.

She went into a dream as the smoke curled around her. She no longer felt pain. She knew she was going to die with her husband and she even felt happy. She walked on through the smoke, past caring. She had been carrying the child on her back. Now her husband took the child.

Finally they came to the Nanshucho Railroad Company property. The fire had destroyed the gate, and they were able to get inside.

Had they found shelter? The fire was still pressing toward them. But here there were concrete walls to hide behind to get out of the reach of the fire dragon. Chiyoko's husband found a *zabuton* that was soaked in river water. He picked it up and managed to protect his wife and child from the furious wind. The air was completely filled with smoke. But finally as the rays of dawn began to creep across the night sky the terrible wind slackened.

The Sakamotos decided it was time to return to their house. On the way they passed scores of dead bodies. They went by the big Ki Bridge. It was entirely burned down, and they saw bodies floating in the river—bodies of people who had been caught on the bridge as it burned.

Finally they reached their home, or what had been their home. It was all ashes. They looked across the Nihonbashi district. A few hours earlier hundreds of houses had clustered there. Now it was a wasteland.

They learned the story of the family next door. As they felt the fire the wife had gone into labor. Halfway through the birth process she began to die. She was terribly burned and crying out in a loud delirious voice before she died.

The child was born filthy and burned in the face but alive; the father swept it up in an overcoat, clutched it to him, and saved it.

Hideyoshi Kaneko was a Buddhist priest who lived in the Fukagawa district. As the bombs were falling he took his wife by the hand and abandoned their burning house, moving into the street. The street was so filled with acrid smoke that they could not see ten feet ahead.

But just off the ground for about a foot, there was no smoke, so they got down and crawled to the shelter of the large concrete building a block away. It was a cable manufacturing plant. They saw an enormous concrete pipe next to the building and crawled into it. Others kept coming and soon there were twenty people clustered in that pipe. They were safe from the flames but the heat was intense.

Kinosuke Wakabayashi was a commander of the civil guard, senior officer for the Sumida district. Weeks earlier, after a suggestion from his superior officer, he had moved his wife and two younger children to the country, to live with relatives in Chiba. Wakabayashi and his teenage daughter, who was in middle school, were the only ones living in their house in Sumida.

When the sirens began, Commander Wakabayashi left his house and began his rounds, making sure that the people in his district had left their houses. When every thing had been checked and he saw that the firestorm had taken over the industrial area, he knew that there was nothing more he could do. The firefighters were nonplused, as were the civil defense workers. It was every man for himself.

Realizing this, Commander Wakabayashi went back to his house and found it burning. He picked up his teenage daughter and began walking toward the Asahi Brewery warehouse on the bank of the Sumida River. Inside the fence around the property he saw that the concrete building with its corrugated steel roof was safe. He and his daughter could not get into the building, which was locked tight, but found shelter against the intense heat in the lee of the building.

They had no food or water, but they were alive. From their vantage point they could see the horror around them, the people streaming toward the Sumida River bridges, and leaping into the river, clothes and even their bodies aflame. Soon both banks of the river were clogged with bodies. The bridges were so hot that anyone who touched a bit of iron or steel was seared like bacon on a grill. The bridges, streets, and rail lines were scenes of death as people dropped from exhaustion and breathed their last gasps of smoke.

After an hour in the lee of the building, Commander Wakabayashi and his daughter ventured around the corner. They heard someone inside the building and began to shout, attracting the attention of the watchman inside. He opened the door for them. Inside was Matsuo Hayashi, another Sumida resident, who had been lucky enough to find the shelter. Looking out the window, Commander Wakabayashi noticed that the tide was turning, and the bodies in the Sumida River, bobbing up and down like logs, were being washed out to sea.

Tatsu Sakai was at home when the firebombs began to rain down on her house near the bank of the Sumida River. Her husband was at work. When she heard the sirens she ran outside to their air-raid shelter, taking her pet cocker spaniel. She crawled in and shut the roof on top of herself.

She crouched in darkness while the firestorm passed. After an hour had gone by, she raised the cover, saw the burning embers of her house, and the houses around it, picked up the dog, and set out to seek shelter. She walked for two hours before finally seeing a large group of people huddled under a bridge, across the Sumida. She went down to join them.

It was a miracle! There she found her husband safe and sound.

Before the bombs rained down on her block, Koike Yoshie had put together a sleeping mat and two quilts. When she heard the bombers overhead, she picked them up, went outside the house and headed for Sumida Park. There she went straight to the pond beside the Meiji Theater. She put her futon down in the shadow of the big stone memorial there, and placed her small son on it.

Chiyoko Yokozawa was in the hospital, and on the evening of March 9 her second son was born. She was alone, as her husband Masaki was in the army. Although he was stationed in Tokyo, he was on duty and couldn't be with her. The baby had just been born when the hospital caught fire, and all the patients were evacuated. Carrying her baby in her arms, Chiyoko Yokozawa set out to save herself.

Still, the B-29s continued to come in to the attack zone and, still, the bombs continued to fall.

Just after the bombing started Hiyoshi Inoue, who lived in a concrete apartment building in Nakagawa Shirogawa, heard the sounds of a large plane overhead and then the sound of a bomb exploding. He looked out the third-floor window and saw fire all around. It seemed as if Tokyo was finished. Because he was chief fire prevention officer, first he checked the neighborhood. The fleeing people had locked their doors.

He heard an angry sound like some evil bird slowly coming lower—a B-29—and after that he felt something cold drop on his skin. It was not oil but it was oily. Clearly, he thought, it was crude oil. And it came from that low-flying B-29, without a doubt.

These drops were not burning, but elsewhere they were burning houses and people. The Americans were dropping gasoline on people!

His perception was almost correct, and it was buttressed by the experience of Juhira Shimizu, who not only felt the liquid but also smelled it and saw it burning. And Shimizu-san noted that the fire could not be extinguished with water.

These were the M-69 cluster incendiaries, each bomb about seven inches long, filled with napalm, a jellied gasoline substance that had strong adhesive power. It was an M-69 cluster that had exploded at the feet of Fire Warden Obata, destroying his face and burning through his shoes to destroy his toes. What Ueno-san and Shimizu-san had experienced was contact with napalm from unexploded bombs

Seizo Hashimoto, although only thirteen years old, was already an old hand at fire fighting. His family had lived in Miyoshi in the Fukagawa district but had been burned out and then moved to Koto—the center of this night's bombing.

Seizo had become separated from his family when the bombs started to fall and found himself alone on Mitsubei Avenue, facing the Omiya Bridge across the Sumida River, the fire on both sides of him. He was terrified. It looked to him like great snake, belching fire and smoke. The smoke was everywhere, although the firestorm had not yet reached him.

He saw a woman taken by the firestorm. She was apparently a courtesan from the geisha quarters, and was wearing a red kimono with gold and silver threads and a gold obi, with a red lotus blossom in her hair. He watched terrified as the storm took her, whipped and twisted her body with its hot tongue, and then turned her into a human torch. A piece of her kimono swirled through the air and dropped at Seizo's feet.

He saw two people emerge from the river, father and child, their bodies dripping wet but saved.

He approached the bridge, which was hot to his feet, but the large central pillar of concrete protected a small area from the wind and fire. He moved into the shadow of the pillar and lay, face down. He was exhausted. He could go no farther.

Twenty-year-old Takeiro Ueba was inside his family's house in Asakusa that evening, studying courses that would lead him to become a teacher in the Tokyo public schools. Also at home were his father, Aichi, his mother, Umeko, his younger brother, Kenjiro, and his younger sister, Ueko. His father was manager of a fishing company.

When the sirens sounded, the radio announced that the planes were coming. Ueba's father was standing in the garden looking at the sky but not yet seeing any planes. Ueba, who was a member of the Young Volunteer Fireman's Association, went outside to attend to his duties. The other family members went to the local park that was their safe area. Their house was on the edge of the burned district but it was not burned, although the third and fourth houses from it were both consumed.

Soon enough the bombs were falling on Asakusa, and young Ueba was in the street fighting the fires with straw mats and sand because the water mains failed.

Tokyo's firemen thought they were prepared to fight the fires, but they found themselves facing entirely new problems. With the first reports, the hose companies headed out, and almost immediately discovered that the firestorm had destroyed water mains. After an hour the firemen had to admit to defeat. Ninety-six fire engines were burned to ashes that night. Eighty firemen were killed; forty were missing, as were five hundred volunteers.

Captain Shigenori Kubota was a doctor and professor of medicine at the Imperial Army School of Medicine in Tokyo's Honjo district. His apartment was in the medical school building in the Imperial Army No. 1 hospital on Meiji Avenue. He was also director of Army Rescue Unit No. 1, which was responsible for all of Tokyo except the Imperial Palace. In this capacity he was responsible for nine doctors (each doctor to head one unit); eleven nurses; four drivers; and four trucks. With this slender force he was supposed to cover all of Tokyo.

Just before sunset on the evening of March 9, Captain Kubota looked out the window. Below him spread a panorama of Tokyo. He could see the blue water of the harbor. It was a pleasant spring evening, although a bit windy, but that was to be expected in March. At 10:30, Captain Kubota looked out his window again but saw nothing but the city sprawl. There was no traffic moving. Something had triggered the sirens. It was probably a lone U.S. B-29; in the last few nights several B-29s had flown over the city, probably checking winds and weather for the next day. B-san, as Tokyo citizens had dubbed the big silver bombers, seemed to be an overblown weapon. The bombers came in the daylight hours at such high altitudes that their contrails were visible long after they had left the scene. So far they had proved to be, as the airmen said, "a weapon we can live with."

But when the sirens blew the rescue squads had to prepare for action, so Captain Kubota went to his command post in the building and made sure that all nine of his units were on alert. Then he watched and waited.

Suddenly he saw the silver shapes of B-29s, and heard the engine noises. They were much lower in the sky than usual. He also saw the eastern area of Tokyo begin to take on a reddish glow—not a bright red, but a rusty color, fire and smoke. The topography of Tokyo was such that fire could spread very quickly; many building fronts were packed three-deep from street to alley. The fires seemed to be spreading quite fast in winds that seemed unusually high. Captain Kubota did not have an anemometer handy but if he had, he would have seen it registering winds of sixty, seventy, and eighty miles per hour.

Captain Kubota watched but did nothing to take action. There was no reason for him to move rescue units about until he knew where they would be going.

Captain Kubota was waiting for orders.

2

To Burn Up Japan

The raid lasted two and a half hours, not counting the handful of stragglers who wandered in like vultures. The bombers came in ragged waves, sweeping over the eastern section of the capital and bringing widespread destruction to the Koto area. A quarter of the vast city burned up. After General Power's plane dropped its bombs, he climbed to ten thousand feet and circled the area, watching as B-29s from the three wings streamed in. He saw small fires start, and almost immediately erupt, flowing into one another, pressed by the high winds until huge areas were in flame. It was an awesome sight.

What impressed Power most was the lack of opposition. The Japanese had been almost completely surprised by this raid. The antiaircraft guns were silent for the most part, and only an occasional fighter rose to challenge the intruders.

Power looked down almost in disbelief as the fires spread into one vast firestorm, leaping across city blocks, firebreaks, and rivers in a rectangle about three miles wide and five miles long. It was hard to control the airplane in the constant buffeting from the updrafts. He watched for half an hour, then looked at his fuel gauges and turned for the Marianas, shaken by what he had seen. His tail gunner reported that he could still see the fires when they were 150 miles from the city.

Back at Guam, General LeMay was waiting. Power had sent one brief message as he went in: "Weather clear. Bombing visually." The rest would have to wait until the planes came home.

"It looks good," the general said, and a smile creased his tired face.

General Power's plane landed on Guam's north field at 8:30 on the morning of March 10. The general had dark circles under his eyes, and he was badly in need of a shave. LeMay had remained in the operations office, waiting for him. "It was a hell of a good mission," Power said.

General LeMay was perfunctory. He was waiting to see the reconnaissance photos and they had not yet come in. Meanwhile, the crews were debriefed as they came back to Guam, Saipan, and Tinian. Fourteen B-29s had been shot down, and forty-two had been damaged.

By the time the Americans returned to their bases, Radio Tokyo was on the air broadcasting news of the "slaughter bombing." The Japanese made no attempt to minimize the damage. The sea of flames that engulfed the residential and commercial sections of Tokyo was reminiscent of the holocaust of Rome caused by Emperor Nero.

It was several days before Tokyo's weather was clear enough to get good photos. When General Le May finally saw them, he called the mission "a diller." The fires burned all night, destroying an area of almost sixteen square miles. Central Tokyo had been destroyed, turned into wasteland overnight; 63 percent of the commercial district had burned, along with the heart of the congested residential district. Only 18 percent of the burned-out area was industrial.

For General LeMay, the most important thing was a message from General Arnold: "The results of yesterday's mission show that your crews have the nerve for anything. Congratulations."

General LeMay was satisfied. His job had been on the line, and now it was safe.

He had a green light to burn up Japan.

3

The Long Day

At 3:40 in the morning, Tokyo area Army Command sent orders to Captain Kubota to take the Rescue Unit No. 1 into action. A staff officer arrived at the Army Medical School building, and told the captain he would not have many medical supplies with which to work. For the past week the supply department had been waiting for medicines and so far they had not come. Particularly missing was penicillin, the most important drug in the anti-infection arsenal.

What was the problem? Captain Kubota knew only too well: transport. Neither trucks nor drivers were available to deliver the supplies. Just today the supply department had sent emergency drivers to pick up medicine from the manufacturers. The war in the Philippines, in Burma, and on Iwo Jima had so decimated the army's air transport that delays were inevitable.

"Shikata ganai!" the staff officer said. "It can't be helped." They would just have to make do with what was available.

At 3:50 A.M. Captain Kubota and his staff left the hospital and got into their command vehicle, an army ambulance. They drove slowly through the deserted streets of the capital city, each of them tense. As they moved from one district to another they could see the bursting flames of what they recognized as the firestorm. It was moving rapidly, throwing fireballs as though they were fireworks for some monstrous celebration.

They climbed Yanagicho Hill, and then Kagura Hill, and hastened to cross Iida Bridge. Until this night the entire area had been virtually undamaged, hit once or twice by stray bombs from some erring American bombardier. But tonight was different. They were passing through a field of desolation.

Captain Kubota drove through smoldering ruins until he reached the Kudanshita army command post. All around him were smoldering fires, still bearing hot embers that burned anything they touched. Smoke from the fires still lingered on the ground. The Miya Mansion of Kaya was completely burned out. Its once splendid tall columns and ornate woodwork now resembled a charcoal caricature, blackened pillars with smoking ruins collapsed around them, standing sentinel in a sea of rubble.

Women and even children of the volunteer corps scurried about in *monpei* and canvas shoes, trying to find survivors amid the rubble and helping them to the aid station. The temperature was near freezing and the workers were shivering as they labored, moving wreckage to reach bodies.

From Kudanshita, they followed a ditch for three thousand yards, the fire on their left. Finally they reached the Itsu Bridge where the last army post was located. An officer emerged from the building next to the bridge to give Captain Kubota his orders.

Army Hospital Rescue Unit No. 1 was ordered to Honjo, in east Tokyo, to rescue injured people. Captain Kubota was to be in charge, although he and his men would work closely with the Honjo civil defense chief.

The staff officer spoke vaguely about private doctors and medical facilities, but this was just social courtesy. Kubota knew very well that nearly all doctors in the Tokyo area had been enlisted in the medical service and that nearly all private medical facilities had been closed. Nothing was said in response to the staff officer's flowery words. The men of Rescue Unit No. 1 tightened their helmets and moved on. At 4:50 they pulled up in front of army headquarters at Honjo. No one was there. They drove on through Ogawa, Suda, and Iwamoto, shaken by the horror they saw around them. They drove eastward, being careful not to be trapped by the still advancing fire.

The devastation was ghastly. Asakusa Bridge was still standing but was aflame and covered with smoke and seemed ready to fall down. The electric and telephone lines around it had collapsed into the street as the poles burned. Live electric wires snaked out across the streets. The hot overhead lines had also collapsed on the rail lines, creating more dangers. The wooden railroad carriages had burned to charcoal, although some of them were still intact. When they had cooled they could be pushed over by a child and would disintegrate.

The streets were full of rubbish, the entrails of hasty flight. Dead horses lay where they had fallen in the streets, and skeletons of handcarts, wagons, and bicycles littered the roads. The twisted and contorted human bodies that lay everywhere told the story of panic, fear, and terror that had overcome this city. Only a few had managed to escape the clutch of the firestorm.

The roads, no longer thoroughfares, were littered with heaps of junk: scraps of steel and glass that could slash tires; pots and pans; futons and clothes; mountains of burned plaster; ragged boards: and all the other debris of a city destroyed. Captain Kubota drove as far as he could, but the wreckage became so thick that finally the ambulance had to stop. Bodies and rubble were everywhere.

The immediate problem: a water main had burst and flooded the road. The sides of the road were such a mass of mangled bodies and debris that the vehicle could not get by. The crew piled out and cleared a path. Captain Kubota picked up the arm of a body and the flesh came away in his hand. The passage clear, they piled back into the ambulance and drove on. As they drove, the night began to end and streaks of light came through the haze and smoke in the eastern sky.

They drove to the Ryogoku Bridge across the Ichido River. They were stunned: countless corpses were everywhere. It was a forest of the dead, extending out from the bridge in every direction. Bodies were crumpled so close together that they must have been touching as they died. They lay there, mute evidence of the fury of the U.S. attack on Tokyo's civilian population.

Captain Kubota looked out over the river and shook his head. What a pitiful sight it was, so appalling that it exceeded his imagination. What could rescuers do? There was no one to rescue. If you touched one of the roasted bodies, the flesh would crumble in your hand. Humanity was reduced to its chemical properties, turned into carbon.

They crossed to the Sumida River and found a scene even more horrifying. Burned bodies and logs blackened the surface of the river as far as the eye could see. Kubota could not make out the difference between bodies and logs, all seared by fire dragon that had passed this way. The bodies were nude, the clothes having been burned away, so there was no way to tell men from women and even children. Charred meat is what the captain saw. And the area was still covered with a thick haze, a remnant of the smoke that had asphyxiated these people even as they jumped into the water, hoping to save themselves.

Captain Kubota's eyes came to rest on the riverbank. The wind was still blowing hard, in fitful gusts. The waves subsided for a moment and the captain saw something that shook him: stacked as though by a machine were rows upon rows of corpses. The machine was the tide that had risen and lowered since the firestorm had passed by. The Sumida River told its own story of disaster. When the heat had become deadly, the mob had rushed like lemmings to the water's edge and leaped in, only to be suffocated by smoke or drowned.

On the other side of the river was more evidence of the tragedy: the National Sports Center, a huge concrete structure, was enveloped in smoke. Captain Kubota knew that inside he would find more mountains of corpses, roasted like so much *yakiniku*.

Next stop was Midori, where the day before had stood a hundred houses. Now ten houses dotted what had overnight become an open field. Nearby was a busy road that ran under an overpass 1,100 meters long. The overpass had collapsed and now the only way to get through was to crawl.

In the heart of Honjo stood a large government office building that had escaped the flames. Captain Kubota looked at the building, with many sad thoughts racing through his mind. How miraculous it was, how strange were the ways of fate, for the firestorm had passed by here leaving that great building untouched, while all around it was rubble. And beneath the rubble or lying twisted on top of it were the seared corpses of the unlucky people who had been in the wrong place at the wrong time.

Captain Kubota drove back to the center of the city and discovered that serious damage had also been sustained in the Asakusa, Honjo, Fukagawa, Kito, and Mukojima wards. Asakusa, with its profusion of entertainment places, geisha houses, whorehouses, restaurants, and bars, had been almost completely wiped off the map. Ninety-nine percent of its houses had been destroyed or rendered uninhabitable. In some places the water mains had burst and water was gushing forth as from a mountain stream. Other areas had no water at all.

Tokyo had been sorely hurt; even the houses and buildings that stood had been changed somehow. The enemy had struck a powerful blow at Japan's major industrial complex. Captain Kubota, like many other Tokyo residents, had been told that Japan could never be bombed. He had believed the honeyed words of the generals. And now the worst had happened.

On he went with his rounds in the ambulance, to the city office in Honjo and then to the district office to see the overworked officials handing out food, blankets, and other necessities of life to refugees.

At 6 A.M. the captain was back on the road, heading west to Kamezawa. Here through the haze and smoke appeared another manifestation of the carnage. All along the roadside lay blackened corpses, victims of asphyxiation. The captain could tell because of the way the bodies were bunched together. The dead here were so numerous and the obstacles in the road so plentiful that the ambulance could travel only at a snail's pace. On the left, he saw another mountain of corpses. The smoke closed in again before he could ascertain the reason for their bunching up. Some sort of building had been there, and the refugees had crowded into it before it had been blasted by the firestorm's heat.

There was no point in going farther; there was nothing to be done for the dead, and the living were Captain Kubota's concern. He headed back to the

Honjo district building for orders, and was told that the National People's School near the Nishiukushu Railroad Station had been designated as the place for his operations. The building was old, but it was made of concrete and seemed fit for the task.

The captain and his crew entered the school's main lecture hall on the ground floor. It was overflowing with refugees who had learned that this was to be a treatment center. Kubota selected one corner of the building, set up a desk and several lines of chairs, and prepared to get to work.

How similar were the faces in that sea of humanity he saw before him! They all bore the same expression of relief—that finally they had reached a place where they could get help. Many had lost limbs, or flesh, or an eye. Blindness was a common affliction, but most of it was temporary, the captain noted with relief, and would go away with cleansing and with rest.

The smoke victims worried Captain Kubota the most. Many of these people would develop pneumonia or other complications and would die within the next few weeks because of the irreparable damage done to their lungs. The captain heaved a sigh as he considered man's inhumanity to man. And then he caught himself up short. This was no time for philosophizing. There was work to be done.

The refugees lined up for medical treatment. There was no way to make order out of the confusion. The most sensible thing would have been to separate them by types of injury, but there were too many wounded and too few caregivers for that.

Almost all the refugees suffered from conjunctivitis, an eye infection, caused by the smoke and hot winds. This was easy to treat. He washed out the eyes with salt water and told them that in a few days their eyesight would return to normal. They were lucky. Most of them had become sleepy in the smoke and had gone to sleep. But they had awakened. The unlucky ones were lying in the streets and roadsides. They hadn't woken up and had been asphyxiated by the smoke.

As Dr. Kubota worked, he questioned his patients. What had happened to them?

Toraji Ono and her two children had been fleeing on the Sumida River Bridge when suddenly it collapsed under them. She and her children jumped into the river; she grabbed onto a log and her children held on to her. Fortunately the water put out the fires in their *monpei*. By keeping their eyes closed they had avoided eye injury.

But Toyuko Tsumano, another homemaker, had spent the whole night stamping out fires on her children's clothing and breathing smoke. Her eyes were so tightly sealed when Dr. Kubota examined her that he thought she was blind.

Next up was Katsuko Yamamoto, and when Dr. Kubota first looked at her he thought she, too, was blind. She lived in a very old house, dating back to the Meiji era, with her extended family: sixteen people in all. Mrs. Yamamoto's personal family consisted of herself and eight children. The eldest, the man of the house, was her nineteen-year-old son. Downstairs they ran a clock and watch business.

When the air-raid siren sounded, the other members of the family went out to the designated place; Mrs. Yamamoto was the last to leave, she thought. Before she could leave, the firestorm swept to their house, and she became trapped. The dirt and dust got into her eyes, and soon she could not see. Then she felt the intense heat and knew she was going to drown in a sea of fire.

She was just about to fling herself through the wall of flame when her eldest son came up to her and handed her a rope, which he used to lead her to the door and out of the burning building. She still could not see, but outside she learned that all her family had survived, and they made their way behind the firestorm and were looking for shelter. When morning came they learned that the school had been designated as a treatment center and traveled there.

Dr. Kubota cleaned out Mrs. Yamamoto's eyes and did a minor operation on the lids. Her sight was saved. "I feel reborn," she said.

So it went all day long. Not all cases ended as happily as Mrs. Yamamoto's did. Many of the people who survived the firestorm died of shock or injuries, and contracted infections that could not be controlled with the meager medicines available.

Others had managed to survive without the help of first aid. Hideyoshi Kaneko, the Buddhist priest, and his wife were among them. After they crawled to the factory and hid in the big pipe, they were sheltered, though the hot winds searched for them. Next morning they tried to find other members of the family. They found Hideyoshi's mother- and sister-in-law alive and well in a shelter. But even after searching for many days, they never found a trace of Hideyoshi's father-in-law. He had, like so many others, simply gone up in smoke.

Hideyoshi and his wife then went across Tokyo to stay with a friend in Bunkyo-ku, near the University of Tokyo's main campus. There, they found that the lucky ones who had not participated in the Dance of the Fire Dragon could not appreciate the terrors of that night. They joked with Hideyoshi about his experiences. "Your wife must be a Negro," they said. "She is so black."

And of course she was, blackened by the breath of the fire dragon. The effect lasted past the end of the war.

Tatsu Sakai, her daughter, cocker spaniel, and husband huddled under the pier of the Sumida River Bridge with scores of other refugees all night long, praying for the dawn to come. Their clothes were burned, their faces blackened, and their souls seared by the breath of the fire dragon, But they had survived.

Koiko Yoshie and her son remained out in the open near the big pond on the grounds of the Meiji Theater throughout the night. All the water was evaporated from the pond by the heat, but she and her son were protected from the fires and embers by their futons. Next morning they felt blessed and gave thanks for their survival.

Takeiro Ueba, who had found sanctuary easily, roused himself the next morning and went to look at his family's house. It was undamaged, which was a miracle. That night, 260,000 houses had burned. All this had been accomplished by fewer than three hundred bombers dropping M-69 incendiary clusters,

To Ueba the impact of the bombing was lost because he and his family had not been directly affected. But later in the day, Ueba went out to survey the damage and to look up a good friend. He did not find the friend because his house had burned down. He was shocked to see the piles of dead people and horses on the Nihonbashi Bridge across the Sumida River. He went to the Asakusa Shrine and found it had burned down. Then the impact of the bombing began to strike.

For a few days Ueba went back to school, but then he was called up by the army and sent to Kumamoto, where he was given virtually no training and assigned to a machine gun squad.

Miwa Koshiba had somehow got through the night in her stinking sewer near the Sumida River. She saved her baby daughter from death three times that night. She devoted as much attention as she could to her six-year-old son, for she could see that he was growing sicker by the hour. Time after time she squeezed out dirty rags and wet them with the filthy sewer water to cool the boy's fever.

Dawn brought little relief. She sat in the sewer, still unable to see. Her eyes were sealed shut by the hot winds that carried gluey grit. Finally in the morning some kind people led her out of the sewer to a place where someone had cooked rice, and she was able to wash her face and clean out her eyes.

Later in the day Miwa decided to take the children back to the school where her husband had stayed with her mother and father. But when she tried to cross the Sumida River she saw that it was impossible. The bridges were piled high with the bodies of those who had been kissed by the fire dragon.

She decided to go upstream to the Hajima Bridge and later in the day she was able to cross it with her three children. No one paid her any attention as she struggled along carrying the baby and sometimes the boy as well. He was half-delirious with fever.

Masatake Obata, the former soldier, was the most knowledgeable of the eight who huddled in the trench beside the streetcar line. He spent the night waking his companions as they drowsed off. "Don't sleep," he said. "Don't go to sleep, or you will never wake up. Go to sleep and you will die."

Finally the last straggling B-29 left the scene. When dawn came, the eight people went their own ways. Obata headed for the Sensoji Hospital, behind the Asakusa Shrine. With his hands stretched out before him, walking as though on roller skates, he staggered on his battered feet to the hospital.

When he got there he asked for medical treatment. He was taken to a doctor who looked him over and took his pulse. A nurse brought burn medicine. They helped him out of his burned clothing and gave him a hospital gown. They treated his burns with ointment and bandaged them. When they had finished Obata resembled an Egyptian mummy, bandages covering his whole body except his eyes. And these were swollen almost shut.

"Where should I take this gentleman?" the nurse asked. "Which ward?"

The doctor considered this for a moment. Then he spoke quietly to the nurse. "It's not necessary to take him to any ward. Take him down to the morgue in the basement. Let him join the other dead. There is no hope."

The doctor didn't know that Obata had overheard him. "I won't die," he said to himself. "I won't! I won't!"

The nurse brought him to the basement, found a mat for him, and helped him to lie down. Then she left. The hours passed, and he lay there, unconscious most of the time. No one came. Occasionally, they brought another body and dumped it unceremoniously. But no one even glanced at Obata. It was as if he were already dead.

On the night of March 9, twelve-year-old Saotome Katsumoto's family heard the first warning about an air raid on the radio news. Then at about 10 o'clock the sirens sounded briefly, but the raid did not materialize and Saotome went back to sleep. When the bombers came at midnight, Saotome and his family went to the Fukagawa Middle School, which was recommended by their block warden, and they were safe there. Saotome put on his long-sleeved protective clothing and although the firestorm reached out to get him several times, he managed to escape its clutches.

But that terrible night Saotome's belief in his government was destroyed, He saw the dreadful results of the firestorm. At the school he and his family looked with new eyes at the big situation maps the teachers had put up on the bulletin boards. Saotome already knew that most of what teachers said was propaganda. After this night he was sure of it and no longer believed that Japan was going to win the war. Saotome's best friends, Mida and Harada, never returned to the school; he was sure they were dead.

Kinosuke Wakabayashi and his daughter spent the night in the Asahi Brewery Warehouse on the bank of the Sumida River. They felt the hot breath of the firestorm but were never in any danger. When morning came they decided to go back to their house and see what had happened to it. They picked their way through the burned vehicles and debris of houses and bodies. When they got to the street where their house had stood, they saw only a pile of rubble and ashes.

Wakabayashi's daughter cried when she picked up her teddy bear. He was lying face down in the pile of ashes that had been her bedroom, covered with charcoal. One paw had been burned off. "Don't cry," her father said. "Think of what it would have been like if we had been here. I will buy you a new bear.

"And look," he said bravely, picking up a twisted piece of glass that had been melted by the firestorm. "Here is your mother's favorite flower vase. See, it will still hold water. We will rebuild our house. But right now we have to build something we can live in. You go and join your mother and the others in the country but I have work to do in Tokyo."

And he began scrabbling through the rubble, picking up a beam here, some unbroken tiles there, a shoji screen, some lengths of pipe. There was nothing left but hope, but he had plenty of that.

From his house in Koiwa, Kenji Moro watched his factory burn to the ground. The next morning he went to Kojima to survey the damage. He made his way through the bodies, across the vast wasteland of the Sumida area, until he came to the place. At first he did not recognize the twisted wreckage, but then he saw the remains of the company truck with the logotype Moro Construction Company, and he knew he was at the right place. It had all been destroyed. But he still had his health and he would start over.

4

Agony

Hampering Captain Kubota's efforts to save lives was the lack of medicines. Even penicillin was in short supply, although Japan's pharmaceutical companies were working hard to meet the demand.

For five years before the beginning of the Pacific war, Japan had been isolated from the scientific and medical developments in the West. Thus, sulfa drugs were virtually unknown in Japan, although almost every Allied soldier had a sulfa packet in his personal gear. But penicillin, which had been overlooked by the Allies, proved to be the wartime wonder drug of Japan.

Alexander Fleming, who lived in London, had discovered penicillin's healing properties in 1928, but it was twelve years before this wonder drug was widely used. When World War II began, the United States and Britain were producing vast quantities of sulfa, the standard treatment for infection.

Japan didn't begin to study penicillin until the fall of 1943. At that time Major Katsuhiko Inagaki, chief of the Army Medical School, found a study of penicillin in a German weekly magazine carried to Japan by a U–boat. That was the beginning of the epoch-making development of antibiotics in Japan. In January 1944, penicillin was introduced to the Japanese public via a newspaper article in *Asahi Shimbun,* which told how penicillin had saved the life of Britain's prime minister, Winston Churchill, whose pneumonia was cured in two days. The article originated in Argentina.

Japanese pharmaceutical companies all cooperated with a government program to produce as much penicillin as possible. In September 1944, mass production of penicillin began in Japan and was well under way when the firebombing campaign started. Japanese doctors and hospitals had access to this drug and used it constantly to treat infections. But to get penicillin, one had first to find a doctor.

If Miwa Koshiba had been able to get penicillin for her son, he would not have been so ill just a few hours after the night they spent in the sewer on the Sumida River. The boy had contracted typhus fever, an illness that penicillin could cure. But in her struggles for safety, Miwa was unable to find medical help, not even a first aid station.

Miwa had lost her shoes sometime during the long night. As she walked along streets where the pavement had retained its heat, her feet grew very sore. When she reached Hajima Bridge the problem grew acute. The bridge was still so hot from the firestorm that she could not cross in her bare feet. So this elegant, cultured woman went back and poked among the bodies until she found a woman who was her size. She took the woman's shoes. They fit very well. Without a whimper she accepted them and made her way with her children across the bridge and toward the school where she hoped her husband and parents were waiting

As she went she inquired of those who passed by, "Where can I get medical attention for my son?" No one seemed to know, so she went on back to the school, which she knew was still standing. The authorities there would help her, she believed.

Satoko Sano and her children remained in the improvised shelter near the school until the all-clear sounded on the morning of March 10. If Satoko's husband had followed the advice given by Japan's propagandists, he would have trudged off through the firestorm to the munitions factory, put in his hours, and given his utmost to the defense effort, despite the threat to his family.

But in truth Sano did not even think about the factory. In the confusion of the firestorm, he had become separated from his wife and children, and spent the long night looking for them. He found them the next morning in the little park where they had taken refuge, one small daughter with her hair burned off, and all three with many burns. They had been lying on the ground with many other wounded and when Sano came up to them, he thought at first that they were all dead. But now there was a joyful reunion.

Even after being reunited with his family, Sano did not think about the factory. He did think about their burns. Satoko had burns on her arms and back where flying embers had hit. The children's burns needed even more attention.

Satoko knew what to do. She persuaded her husband to go to Nanamo, her hometown, which was famous for its *onsen* (hot springs). But Nanamo was twenty kilometers away.

Getting to Nanamo was difficult. The ships on the Sumida River had burned up. The trains were overcrowded. The buses and streetcars were not running. The only way to get to Nanamo was to walk. So walk they did, the children barefoot, Satoko in *tabi* (split socks) and *geta*, the wooden sandals that nearly everyone wore. Satoko's relatives took them in, and every day the family bathed in the hot springs. The warm, soothing waters cured their burns and the little girl's hair began to grow back.

On March 12, Obata's brothers came to the area to search for him and his family. All they found was the spot where his house had stood before the firestorm. The civil defense authorities had no idea where he or his wife and children were. They had obviously wandered out of the park that night and been devoured by the fire dragon, the authorities said.

His mother, who lived in Kojima-cho, near Ueno Park, came to search, too. She had a feeling that her son was still alive. She went to Sensoji Hospital and checked the records. He was listed as an almost certain fatality, but when the doctor had asked his name, his broken answer had been misheard as Ogata, and that is how he was listed.

Even so his mother sensed he was somewhere around the hospital. She toured the building, calling out his name. Nobody responded. Finally she looked down the basement stairs. "What's down there?" she asked.

"Only the hospital morgue. That's where we keep dead bodies until they are cremated," she was told.

Obata's mother insisted on seeing the basement and a nurse brought her down. She came down calling Obata's name and he tried to answer. He raised himself up on his straw mat, a ghostly figure, swathed in bandages, and tried to answer her. But all that came out was a croak. Still she embraced him. She knew who he was.

Mrs. Obata persuaded the doctor to treat him and release him to her. She went to his factory, which was damaged but had not burned down, and found some of the employees. She arranged for them to come to the hospital with a bicycle cart and a stretcher, and they took Obata to her house on the other side of Tokyo. When they got there, she called her doctor. He came, took one look at Obata, and said "*Gomen nasai.* I am sorry. This case is beyond my experience."

Obata's brothers then decided that Obata should go to a military hospital. They took him down to the central Tokyo railroad station. He arrived on a stretcher, bandaged from head to toe. "Sorry," said the railroad authorities. "We don't sell tickets to dead men."

The Obata brothers then remembered a military ordnance officer in charge of procurement, with whom they had done business in the past, and told him the story.

"This is ridiculous," he said. "Of course Obata-san is a valued supplier. He should have military treatment." He insisted that the railroad authorities put Obata on a train for Murata, where there was a military hospital. One of his brothers accompanied the sick man.

5

Imperial Tour

At the Imperial Palace behind its moat in the heart of Chiyoda district, the emperor heard dreadful rumors about what had happened in the capital city. Chiyoda had not been hit that night; besides, the emperor's palace was supposed to be sacrosanct, guaranteed by the highest Allied authorities against attack.

The emperor insisted on going out into the city to view the damage. The Imperial household officials were aghast. The emperor should not see what had happened, as it was too dreadful for his eyes. They tried to persuade him to give up his plan. But Hirohito would not give up, and when he set his mind on something he would have his way.

So the Imperial caravan drove across the moat and out into the city. The emperor was dressed as an army general, with brightly polished brown boots and an immaculate uniform.

Hirohito decided his first stop would be on the banks of the Sumida River, where he had heard that the worst had happened. When the caravan arrived, Hirohito got out of the Imperial limousine and looked at the scene of destruction. It had been cleaned up by this time, the bodies removed, and a refugee camp of tents and shacks had been set up in an open spot. But the scene was still pretty indicative of the disaster and the remnants of the burned buildings offered proof of the firestorm that had ravaged the area.

The emperor stopped to talk to some people. There was really nothing to be said; all he could offer were vague condolences. The people were surprised that the man who had been declared to be a god would take such trouble for mere mortals. He looked at the people in their rags, with the scorch of the firestorm still on them. Then he got back in his limousine and drove on.

He stopped at another refugee camp, and then went back to the seclusion of the Imperial Palace. But the word was soon on the grapevine that His Majesty had come, and that he had seen and he had cared. The refugees were deeply moved.

As for Hirohito, he was shocked as never before by the extent of the damage. He was convinced now that the war was lost, and he must begin efforts to end it, in spite of the recalcitrance of his generals. They were determined to fight to the end but Hirohito could now see what the end would be: a Japan that was mutilated beyond recovery.

He returned to the palace determined to find a plan of action.

6

Ready for Round Two

After Mission No. 40, on the morning of March 10, 1945, General Curtis LeMay surveyed the results. His photo planes returned from a still-smoking Tokyo. His bombers had wiped out more than fifteen square miles of the city and had killed more than 100,000 people. LeMay wasn't concerned with that. What was important was that they had found a way to destroy Japan's industrial potential, by destroying its cities. True, the United States had lost fourteen B-29s that night, which was not a low figure, but the results made these losses acceptable.

There would be one change for the next mission: the bombers would be allowed to carry some of their machine guns. The element of surprise had now been lost and the bombers could expect more opposition. One plane of the 73rd Wing had been shot down over Tokyo. The Japanese had probably examined the wreckage and learned that the bomber carried no machine guns.

The 314th Wing had suffered the most losses—eight of the forty-nine planes that had reached the target area had not returned. They were the last unit to arrive on the scene, and by the time they began bombing the element of surprise had long since vanished. The city was on fire.

The photo planes returned to the Marianas with their evidence. The pilots and crew could not see the pile of bodies from that altitude but they would not have recognized them anyhow. The bodies had lost all semblance of humanity. When the developed pictures were brought to General LeMay, he took one look and exclaimed, "We've got them!"

The photographs showed that nearly all the buildings in the targeted area had been destroyed, including twenty-three buildings that were designated as military targets. Photo interpreters studied the photographs and concluded that hundreds of vehicles had been destroyed, and most of the buildings still standing had been gutted.

Many questions had been asked about this new technique of firebombing. In General LeMay's mind, nearly all of them had been answered.

The use of Pathfinder aircraft dropping hundred-pound M-47 Napalm bombs to start marker fires had proved to be effective. So had the use of six-pound M-69 incendiary bombs in multibomb clusters with delayed opening fuses. The saturation of 250 tons of bombs per square mile had worked just right. The overall effect had been devastating, and when added to the natural effect of the high winds and cross currents to start the firestorm, the attack had been the most successful bombing mission of the Pacific war.

On the evening of March 10 the future seemed clear at the XXI Bomber Command on Guam. Three more raids were planned. Nagoya, Japan's third largest city and the center of the aircraft industry, was next. The machine gunners would be reassigned to the bombers with strict orders not to shoot anything except searchlights and fighters.

And then General LeMay made a serious error: he began to tinker with the bombing pattern.

7

Nagoya

Nagoya had been bombed in 1942 by the Doolittle raiders. Virtually no damage was done, except to the national ego, which was so sorely bruised that Japan launched a punitive campaign in central China that cost more than 200,000 lives. Since the B-29s had come to the Marianas in 1944, Nagoya, because of its airplane factories, had been a primary target.

Nagoya was sometimes called Mitsubishi City, because its dominant industry was military aircraft, and Mitsubishi was the most important manufacturer. The company manufactured fourteen types of aircraft, several of them new, for the Japanese army and navy. The aircraft engine plants accounted for 40 percent of Japanese engine production.

These first high-altitude raids were not very rewarding for the Americans. Despite many raids called "successful," the Mitsubishi airframe and engine factories had been scarcely touched. However, high-explosive bombs had destroyed many houses and buildings.

Expecting further raids, the Nagoya city government had built the best civil defense system in Japan. Fire lanes had been cut through the city. As with Tokyo, Nagoya was divided into wards for political purposes, and in block associations for defense purposes. The block associations provided buckets, flails, and mats for fire fighting. The public was warned to build cisterns and maintain a supply of water at all times.

The chief of fire fighting of the National Police Agency suggested in a newspaper interview that the effects of bombing could be overestimated.

It is doubtless true that our houses of wood and paper, as foreigners term them, are at a disadvantage in air raids. But with training and courage, why should they be feared?

Fire, wherever it originates, will always run up the paper walls to the ceiling. Provided it is then prevented from going higher by a partition of earth, tin, or even of wood, above the ceiling, it can then be checked there with water. If, however, it brings the ceiling down and gets onto the roof, it will at once spread everywhere and the whole building will be enveloped in flames.

What the citizen must do, the authorities said, was to remove from the house all flammable objects, before the bombing begins. When the air-raid sirens begin to sound, that is the time to take down the *shoji,* the screens that provide partitions between rooms. It is also time to clear the cupboards. If there is no time for such action, the *shoji* and other combustibles should be smashed so they will not provide fuel for fires.

The best way to put out a fire is to stamp it with mats—smother it, authorities said. But if the fire has progressed too far, then it is time to use buckets of water. That's where the neighbors come in. The efforts of three families with water buckets would be enough to control a fire until a fire engine can arrive, authorities said. This theory, of course, suggested that only one family in three would be affected.

In the summer of 1944 the Mitsubishi factories were taken over by the Munitions Ministry. Thereafter the work force changed significantly. Most of the men who had worked at Mitsubishi had been drafted, and so women of the Volunteer Corps were called up for factory duty. By the end of 1944 Japan was a fully mobilized society and in that sense there were no more civilians, a fact that lent some credence to the U.S. claim that burning Japan was morally defensible because every Japanese was engaged in the war effort. The Japanese government's "total mobilization" meant just that, the U.S. military said, adding that there was no way to separate the civil population from the military. So as it was in Tokyo, six-year-old boys and pregnant mothers had to take their chances along with everyone else.

On December 4, the B-29s had returned to bomb the Mitsubishi Engine Factory No. 4. Not much damage was done to the factory by the high-altitude raid, but three hundred workers were killed. Five days later the B-29s returned and another three hundred workers died. Four more high-altitude raids followed, splattering high-explosive bombs throughout Nagoya.

By December 13, Mitsubishi Engine Factory No. 4 had been bombed seven times and 2,800 people had been killed. On January 3, 1945, the bombers came again, this time with a combination of high explosive and incendiary bombs. Only seventy people died in that raid, but 3,500 houses were burned.

Then came General LeMay's new effort: to burn up Japan. On March 11, from the three main Marianas Islands came 307 B-29 Superfortresses, loaded with thousands of incendiary cluster bombs. Their destination was Nagoya, but not specifically Mitsubishi Engine Factory No. 4. These bombers were ordered to set the city aflame and to start another firestorm.

The 73rd Wing sent 134 B-29s, the 313th provided 111, and the 314th Wing sent forty-two. Into the night the bombers headed, steering northwest. They droned on, hour after hour. Eighteen B-29s dropped out because of mechanical difficulties, but the remainder began to fly over Nagoya at 12:20 on the morning of March 12.

The bomb load pattern was the same as for the Tokyo attack. The Pathfinder planes carried hundred-pound napalm bombs to start fires that would light the way for the rest. The planes that followed carried the M-69 cluster bombs.

In examining the results of the Tokyo raid, General LeMay had grown greedy. He decided that bombs had been wasted on areas already burning, and so for the Nagoya raid he ordered the intervalometer setting for the M-69 bombs increased from fifty to one hundred feet.

To avoid collisions, the three bombardment groups approached the target from different altitudes: one group from 4,000 to 4,500 feet, the next at 5,000 to 5,500 feet, and the third at 7,000 feet. They headed first for Iwo Jima to check radar and radios. Then they headed for Nagoya Bay, the most direct route to Nagoya. Each plane was on its own, the captain controlling the flight and the bombing. Down below were U.S. submarines, destroyers, and destroyer escorts ready to move in and pick up any downed aircrews.

Shortly before midnight the air-raid sirens at Nagoya began, calling on civilians to prepare for defense. Radio Tokyo began broadcasting warnings and giving information. Two hundred heavy antiaircraft guns were alerted, as were fifty searchlight installations, and the fighter bases in the area were warned to be ready to send planes to intercept the bombers.

The Americans were not the only ones experimenting with new devices. The Japanese army was preparing to launch half a dozen barrage balloons, set at various altitudes, in hopes that some of the B-29s would run afoul of their cables.

The B-29s came in over the Shima peninsula, beginning at 12:20 A.M. The first of them bombed at six thousand feet, approaching at various angles and singly or in small groups, so the searchlights could not get a bead. The attack was conducted in much the same way as the bombing of Tokyo two nights earlier. The Japanese defenders were not very aggressive; although some of them tried to ram the bombers, none succeeded.

That, however, did not prevent Imperial General Headquarters from making extravagant claims. They had destroyed twenty-two B-29s, the communiqué claimed, and damaged sixty others. There was no truth in the claim, but it did not stop the propaganda.

Several of the B-29s missed Nagoya and bombed the Kii peninsula or the Shikoku area. But most were on target. They burned 25,000 houses that night. *Chunichi Shimbun,* the big Nagoya newspaper, referred to the bombing as a "burning hell," but the newspaper exaggerated. As a military operation, this first Nagoya fire raid was a failure. There were no high winds over Nagoya, there was no firestorm, and it turned out to have been a mistake to reset the intervalometer; the penetration was sharply decreased.

There was another reason for the failure of the U.S. attack. The Nagoya city government had been far more aggressive than Tokyo in its fire defenses. Many fire lanes had been prepared in the city's industrial district. Besides that, the shape of the Nagoya industrial section was quite different from that of Tokyo. Here there was no great sprawling metropolis, but a tightly centered industrial area, and most of the factories had some protection against fire.

Still, from the standpoint of the people of Nagoya, the firebombing was terrorizing; 2,700 people—the vast majority of them women and children, homemakers and schoolchildren—were killed, most of them burned to death in their houses or trying to escape or fight the flames. As the Japanese had already discovered in the Tokyo fire raid, there were no more noncombatants in Japan.

The fire raid on Nagoya roused the Japanese Information Bureau, which managed civilian communication and was an important source of information in Japan, second only to the communiqués of the Imperial Headquarters. This agency was also responsible for censoring civilian newspapers. After the attack, the Information Bureau erupted in fury against the U.S. firebombing and General LeMay. "Worse than the burning of Rome by Nero," the information bureau proclaimed.

There was reason for the government's concern. During the high-altitude bombings, absenteeism at the Mitsubishi factories had been minimal. But after the first fire raid on Tokyo, the figures shot up. Ultimately they would hit 40 percent.

The army could say all it wanted about the fury the firebombings aroused in the hearts of the Japanese people, but the fact was, as the chief editorial writer of the *Nippon Times* put it, the people were deeply impressed with the fire raids. Even now, as the scope was broadening, word of the Tokyo raid was spreading across the country. What sped the news was the evacuation of people from the nation's capital.

The Tokyo raid showed the futility of Japan's civilian defense efforts. Even as the bombers struck Nagoya, the Tokyo authorities were burning the midnight oil, still treating the victims of the bombing, handing out emergency supplies, and finding housing for the one million people who were now home-less. Japanese authorities faced a hopeless task.

One of the odd side effects of the disaster was the placement of some refugees in the better districts of Tokyo that had not yet been hit by bombing. Instead of arousing feelings of gratitude, the encounters left the people of the industrial districts—slums as it were—with deep feelings of resentment. They were unhappy to discover that the people who lived in better districts, such as Chiyoda and Meguro, were not suffering from the general war shortages as much as they. And they did not like it.

Criticism of the military erupted for the first time in the war. Why couldn't the army air force break up the B-29 raids before they began? Why couldn't the government provide decent air-raid shelters for its citizens, the way Britain had managed to do? These questions were not answered, and by the end of the first week after the Tokyo raid the people had even stopped asking. It was no use.

Shikata ganai! It can't be helped!

The government had gambled, and it had lost. The major reason no air-raid shelters had been built was the arrogance of General Tojo, Japan's prime minister until the fall of Saipan. Tojo had promised that Japan would never be bombed.

Outside the military the unthinkable was now becoming common. More and more people, including the emperor, now believed that Japan had no chance of winning the war, and that there was a very good chance that the nation might be destroyed.

8

Searching

Those few who reached the army rescue squad or other medical facilities were lucky; hundreds of thousands struggled to survive without medical treatment, or even elementary first aid.

It took Miwa Koshiba three days to reach the school, where she discovered to her relief that her parents and her husband had survived. But the problem was little Aiyawa, who was obviously very ill with typhus. That very day the whole family started out for the hot springs at Gifu. Doctors could be found at Gifu, and perhaps penicillin, and the hot springs had remarkable curative powers.

The family started out for the main Tokyo railroad station. They walked, of course, as there was no other form of transportation. Miwa's husband carried her mother, and Miwa carried Aiyawa, who was delirious with fever. They had a long wait for a train on the Tokkaido line, for half of the people in Tokyo seemed to have the same idea. Eventually, after several hours, a train arrived. They had been standing near the front of the line, so they managed to get seats. Since the raids on March 9, there had been no express trains, and the progress on this local train was agonizingly slow; they stopped at every station, heading west.

While on the train Miwa's mother suddenly coughed, put her hand to her heart, and slumped over, dead from a heart attack. And before they reached Gifu, little Aiyawa died in his mother's arms.

Once at Gifu station, Miwa's husband solved the problem of what to do with two bodies. But to his dying day, he would never discuss what he had said or done to convince a man to take the bodies away in a handcart. The remaining family members went to their favorite *Onsen* and after several weeks were able to join Miwa's brother-in-law in Nikko, where they spent the remainder of the war.

After the difficult winter of 1945–46 Miwa's husband resumed his business affairs by selling some property. He prospered during the U.S. military occupation, and when he died in 1983, he left a large fortune and two manufacturing companies, which Miwa took over. They were living comfortably then in a large house in Chiyoda-ku and Miwa had jewels and other luxuries. But she still bore scars of that terrible night in the sewer, and the agonizing memories of the death of her son.

During an interview in the summer of 1986, Miwa recalled that what frightened her most was the sight of the B-29s coming down to turn their machine guns on the Japanese civilians as they fled. However, there was no machine gunning that night, because none of the bombers carried machine guns or ammunition.

But Miwa did not believe this and died believing she had seen the machine guns. What happened to her in those terrible early morning hours of March 10 was seared into her soul. She could talk about her own tragedy quite easily, except when she thought about the machine-gunning. . . .

Masatake Obata was moved to the military hospital outside Murawa. Hospital authorities were very leery about taking him in, especially after they looked at his ruined face, with a broken jaw, the gristle of the nose exposed, and no lips or chin. They obviously agreed with the original doctor's diagnosis that he was one of the walking dead. Obata's brothers called on an oral surgeon, but he refused to accept the case because he was sure Obata was going to die.

The brothers said they expected Obata might die, and would not hold the hospital responsible. They insisted the hospital take him as a patient and pulled every string they could with the military procurement authorities. When the doctors said they didn't have the medicines to treat Obata, the brothers said they would get what was needed.

They called the army ordnance offices again, and an army doctor came to the hospital, got a list of items needed to treat Obata, and secured all the medicines, including penicillin, at National Army Hospital in Tokyo. Then began the long work of building a new face for Obata, with bone and skin grafts and dozens of operations.

By the summer of 1986, Obata had recovered as well as he ever would from his encounter with the fire dragon. His face was scarred but presentable. His hair had grown back in patches, because of the scar tissue. His left hand was a claw, his right more normal. He had no toes on his feet, leaving him with a bouncing gait.

After the war, Obata had turned his business over to his brothers and focused on getting government assistance for the victims of the U.S. fire-bombing. The government established programs after the war to help victims of the atomic-bomb attacks on Hiroshima and Nagasaki. But no similar aid was given to victims of the fire dragon. Obata would devote the rest of his life to their cause.

For the next few days after the bombing on March 9, the Army Rescue Unit continued its work at the Honjo National People's School near the Kinshicho station, setting up what was in fact an emergency hospital.

This old three-storied building with classrooms and lecture halls had been rebuilt after the great Tokyo earthquake and fire of 1923. Soon one corner of a lecture hall was turned into a clinic, by moving chairs and desks around. Relief could be seen in the faces of refugees who were lined up, waiting for treatment. These people had just spent a hellish night fleeing from fire and smoke. They had seen such pain and trouble that the taste of this night would not be easily wiped from their memories. Their faces were black with smoke and soot. Many of them were wounded and were in need of treatment.

Dust, dirt, and soot filled red and painful eyes of those suffering from conjunctivitis. The first-aid workers washed out their eyes with salt water, removed the foreign matter, and gave them eye drops.

The dirt had filled the nostrils of some people, causing them to nearly suffocate. Some suffered headaches from the panic, excitement, loss of sight, and similar problems.

As the people waited for the rescue workers to treat them, they formed a line that snaked about as if through a maze. As rescue workers treated them, they talked excitedly about their experiences, their words tumbling out.

In Fukagawa Hirano-cho, Toraji Ono's wife, Toyo, and their son were crossing the bridge with many other people when the bridge suddenly folded up like a fan. Many people were killed, but Toyo and the boy leaped into the river and managed to catch a floating log. They clung to the log, and ducked their heads under the water to avoid the fire and smoke. They nearly drowned. Toraji, however, spent the long night defending their house from the fire, and worrying about his wife and child.

Toraji had suffered so much from the smoke that he could not open his eyes. Toyo took him by the hand and led him to the aid station. She said prayerfully to the doctor, "He was blinded while saving us."

At about 8 o'clock in the morning, new victims of near-suffocation began to arrive. They were brought in, ragged and exhausted from the smoke, sleeping, covered with blankets, their faces pale from trauma and dark with soot. They had lost or were losing consciousness. They did not seem to be breathing, and their pulse was faint to the touch.

When Captain Kubota put his stethoscope to the chest of a twenty-five-year-old woman, he heard a weak but regular heart beat. However he could not hear her breathing. He gave her oxygen and then checked her blood pressure, which was 82/40 (normal blood pressure is in the range of 120/65). His diagnosis: smoke inhalation and carbon-monoxide poisoning.

Rescuers worked hard to help the people, offering oxygen, resuscitation, and strong heart stimulants. The Japanese Army Medical Corps had invented a camphor shot that was very successful, and the doctors also gave injections of a grape sugar solution.

Doctors and nurses working under Lieutenant Kimura began to give victims intravenous injections. One problem was getting the IV needles into the arms properly. Head Nurse Yoshida had a solution that proved effective: she soaked a towel in hot water and applied it to the arm before inserting an IV.

As victims of the worst disaster ever inflicted on Tokyo arrived, doctors and nurses spread medical school blankets over their backs. They worked frantically, with sweat streaming from their faces, to keep people alive with cardio-pulmonary resuscitation. This was heavy labor.

Dr. Kubota tried to assess the physical damages brought on by the firestorm, including burns, near suffocation, carbon monoxide poisoning, and conjunctivitis. Almost all the victims suffered hideous burns on their heads and faces. Many people were missing body parts; legs, hands, arms, and fingers had been burned off. Some had first-degree burns, which were red; second-degree burns, with bruising and blistering; third-degree burns, with damaged tissue; and fourth-degree burns, which left carbonized and blackened tissue—real destruction.

Many victims had fourth-degree burns. It is rare, Captain Kubota said, for people who have burns covering 30 percent of their body to recover. People who suffer burns over 40 percent of their body almost always die. Most of the people who were burned over 40 percent of their body never made it to the first-aid station, he said.

9

Treating the Wounded

Captain Kubota was particularly concerned about the old people who came into the treatment center. These old people were mostly suffering from fevers of 38 degrees C. (100.4 degrees F.) and higher. After examining several of them, he was sure many would develop pneumonia. Most of the old people who contracted pneumonia in those days died. Under the conditions of the firebomb attack, many others also died of shock.

Oxygen and heart medications were given immediately to the older people. But without penicillin, there was little more the medical officials could do. Most of the old people would die.

Still, from all the affected areas, firebombing victims continued to pour in. Time passed. And the work of trying to save a city went on.

During the morning after the bombing, the sick in the treatment center began to regain a sense of tranquility. And more stories were told.

In Asakusa Kondo Cho on that fateful morning the shops were doing business as usual. A nineteen-year-old boy was out in the street at about 12:30 when the bombing began. Strong winds forced people toward the Sumida River and the three bridges in that area: Kototoi Bridge, Azuma Bridge, and, downstream, Umaya Bridge.

This teenager thought he could swim to safety, so he jumped into the river and swam crazily, the fire all around him and sparks falling like snow. Many people drowned, but luckily he found something to hold on to. It was a bunch of straw coming from upstream. "Buddha, I held onto that bunch of straw," he said.

He swam and floated down the river to Kototoi Bridge. There, his good luck did not last. "The bunch of straw fell apart," he said. "I didn't have a life preserver so I had to swim again, but I had no energy left. And then I realized I touched something. It was a buoy that had floated down river from the equipment shop that was burning near Azuma Bridge. A very good idea hit me under the hellish conditions . . . I didn't know when my arms would give out, but if I could hold onto that buoy . . ."

So he reached down, undid his belt, and used it to fasten his body to the buoy. He floated down the river then. When he came to the firestorm's wall of flame, he ducked his head under the surface and bobbed up and down.

"It was hard to breathe, but I managed, and then the dawn came and in my reflection in the water I saw I had blood all over my head. My face was burned and swollen. I felt a stinging pain in my face and neck, because of the dirt in the river. All I saw around me was dead bodies.

"I grew dizzy and I fainted away. When I regained consciousness, I was lying on the riverbank. I had been rescued by somebody near Umaya Bridge."

An injured man who looked like a drowned rat managed to stagger into the aid station; he had learned of its existence at the Ryogoku subway station. How had he become so wet? the people at the aid station asked. How had he been injured? He talked freely but people couldn't understand him. He was suffering from intense shock.

His mind wandered. He was covered with blood. His hair was all burned off; his face was red with second-degree burns. Under a doctor's questioning he revealed that he had been hit by a piece of metal. The wound had not bled and he had carefully removed the fragment with a pair of tweezers. It was surprisingly easy to pick out, he said; his skull was especially hard. At first out of courtesy, he disparaged his injuries. He had used only *banoru gaze* (a sort of gauze smeared with yellow ointment, used to treat minor cuts and bruises).

But doctors saw that his injuries were severe indeed. White zinc oxide paint had burned his eyes, nose, mouth, ears, and head. Before he left the first-aid station his head was completely covered with bandages so that he resembled an Egyptian mummy. The nurses gave him a shot of grape glucose solution and a tetanus vaccination. The danger was that complications would set in.

He did not know that the piece of metal that he picked out of his head was either a shell fragment from one of the firebombs or from a Japanese antiaircraft gun. Aside from the dirt the fragment might have picked up in transit, the metal of the shell and bomb casings had poisonous properties.

One man waiting for treatment was wounded in the face and had a hole the size of a hen's egg in his right hip that was bleeding profusely. The man, who was wearing the trousers of a National People's School uniform, had been fleeing the holocaust from Ohiracho 1 chome when he was wounded by a fragment of an antiaircraft gun shell.

He was pretty bloody but the bleeding had stopped and his condition did not seem to be getting any worse. His facial wound was very black and dirty. His pulse was regular and his color was good. Captain Kubota cleaned the dirt out of the facial wound, and then probed it with an instrument. Five centimeters below the surface he touched what appeared to be a shell fragment. In army medical school they taught that in war, when faced with cases like this, the wounded should be evacuated to the rear and the shell fragment removed.

Dr. Kubota would have to operate. After preparing for the operation, he pulled up several desks and made an operating table. The patient was placed on the table, the wound was disinfected, and novocaine was administered to deaden the pain.

Captain Kubota made an incision about two centimeters at top and bottom to widen the wound. Then he took up a hook and tried to ease the fragment out. It would not move. There was not much bleeding, so he cut deeper until he arrived at the fragment. He searched the wound with his thumb, and when he encountered a shape, he knew he had found the fragment. There were no rules concerning how to bring it to the surface. He considered the best way to pick out the fragment, which was notched. He asked for a forceps and tried to move the fragment, but it would not move.

The patient became restless, complaining of pain from his right leg and toes. Captain Kubota picked up a pair of curved scissors and separated the shell fragment from the surrounding tissue, then pulled and peeled the tissue away from the fragment. The patient did not feel any pain as the fragment was taken out.

What had begun as an easy operation had developed into a difficult one. Another operation was needed to close the gaping hole in the man's rump, but Captain Kubota postponed the second procedure, because of the shock and loss of blood from the first one. He didn't believe the patient could stand the shock of the second operation. The hip looked worse, but the facial injury had been the more dangerous.

So it went, hour after hour, as the doctors tried to save the city, and the military and civil authorities tried to pull themselves together.

10

Propaganda and Facts

After the raid of March 9, the Japanese Cabinet met in emergency session to address the matter of the U.S. firebombings. The success of the air raid on Tokyo had convinced the government that General LeMay intended to burn up all Japan's cities—and their civilian populations.

Censorship was relaxed to permit editorial comment by the newspapers about the raids. Here is Radio Tokyo's comment:

America has revealed her barbaric character before in the terror bombings of civilian populations in Hamburg, Berlin, and other German cities, in her destruction of priceless monuments in various parts of Europe, in her sinking of innumerable hospital ships, and in countless other acts of savagery beyond mention. But the raids on Tokyo and Nagoya within the last few days have demonstrated more spectacularly than ever the fiendish character of the American enemy.

For these recent raids have been the most unquestionable examples of calculated terror bombing. Raining flaming incendiaries over a vast area of civilian dwellings, the raiders can make no excuse of having aimed at military or industrial installations.

It was an attempt at mass murder of workers and children who had no connection with war production or any activity directly connected with the war. There can be no other result than to strengthen the conviction of every Japanese that there can be no slackening of the war effort.

The action of the Americans is all the more despicable because of the noisy pretensions they constantly make about their humanity and idealism. They are the first to accuse others of atrocities, raising loud protests over claims of alleged Japanese mistreatment of prisoners of war [the Bataan Death March] and alleged Japanese destruction in the zones of hostility [The Rape of Nanking]. But even the most extravagant of the false American charges against the Japanese pale into insignificance beside the actual acts of deliberate American terror against civilian populations. No one expects war to be anything but a brutal

business, but it remains for the Americans to make it systematically and unnec-
essarily a wholesale horror for innocent civilians.

Radio Tokyo knew who was responsible for the fire raids—the same man
who had burned up Hamburg—Major General Curtis E. LeMay. "Owing to
unfortunate circumstances, the storm of fire caused by the incendiaries swept
whole districts that were burned to the ground, only here and there were blackened walls of the rare stone buildings left standing." And Radio Tokyo promised that the Japanese will to fight on had been strengthened.

On that day the cabinet ordered the immediate dispersal of civilians from
the Tokyo, Yokohama, Osaka–Kobe, and Nagoya regions. Only essential
workers would remain in the big cities. All others would move out to the countryside.

Perhaps stung by the charge of hypocrisy, or perhaps trying to respond to
U.S. critics (of which the most highly placed was Admiral Chester W. Nimitz)
of General LeMay's new program, the Americans began warning the Japanese civilians to stay out of the cities. Before the next bombing they addressed
Osakans by leaflet. Hundreds of thousands of leaflets were dropped; 82,000
of them were picked up by the police or turned in by citizens, because pos-
session of such a leaflet was a crime. How many were read but not turned in
is unknown, but it seems certain that most Osakans were aware that the bombers had targeted this big manufacturing center.

After the negative experience of Tokyo in trying to find emergency housing for the 800,000 people made homeless in the first Tokyo fire raid, orders
were issued by the Home Ministry: no more private charity. All evacuees must
go to schools, temples, and public buildings.

The effect of the bombing on the general public was electric, although never
admitted by government officials. The official line was strength through joy:
"Now that our houses have been burned down we can fight with complete
freedom." But nobody in his right mind believed that. The generals were grasp-
ing at straws.

The Japanese military tried to show on paper why the B-29 program was
unsound. Up until January 1945, 1,350 B-29s had raided Japan. Of these, the
Japanese claimed either to have shot down or damaged 424 Superfortresses
in Japan; thirty-one B-29s in Manchuria; and twenty more in Singapore.

Assuming that fifty B-29s were lost on their flights to Japan and 181 were
destroyed or damaged in the Japanese raids on the Marianas, the total of B-
29 losses was 706; the personnel loss was 5,775 airmen.

A Superfortress cost $750,000. The Americans had lost $529.5 million. In
working hours this translated into a month and a half's work by ten factories

with ten thousand workers on ten-hour shifts. The Superfortress program was threatening the U.S. war effort, the Japanese propagandists claimed.

In their search for euphoria in the midst of misery the Japanese began to play the "What if" game. Here is how it went:

What if the Americans ran out of B-29s?

The Boeing plant in Seattle, Washington, manufactured 135 B-29s per month. Postulate that thirty-five planes were lost each month due to wear and tear and accidents between Seattle and the Marianas. That reduced the number of B-29s delivered to the XXI Bomber Command to one hundred.

Ten planes, just ten percent, were put out of action by Japanese attacks on the Marianas. That reduced the number to ninety B-29s.

The Americans raided Japan six times per month, and on each raid they lost fifteen planes, or ninety planes per month, the equivalent of the monthly production. Starting with three hundred planes, their losses equaling production, and postulating 5 percent operational losses from metal fatigue and other difficulties, that is a loss of fifteen planes per month. That means that in twenty months the Americans would run out of B-29s. And if the Japanese defenders could increase their kills by 20 percent or three planes per month . . . and so on and so forth.

The problem with that reasoning was that U.S. production was increasing, not falling off. The Japanese raids on the Marianas had come from Iwo Jima, which had now been captured and was a U.S. air base and an emergency landing field for the B-29s, reducing the loss of aircraft. The increasing activity of air-sea rescue units and U.S. submarines saved many aircrews after their planes were ditched.

So all the manufactured statistics and euphoric dreams came to naught, and what remained was the grim truth about the LeMay program. If the war went on much longer, he would indeed burn up the cities of Japan.

LeMay was riding the crest of the wave. Word of the enormously successful Tokyo raid had made it to the Joint Chiefs of Staff and silenced the criticism of Admiral Nimitz and lesser lights. General LeMay was planning his third and fourth raids, Osaka and Kobe, and he had plans to start taking on the lesser cities, too.

11

The First Osaka Fire Raid

Before the war Osaka was the most densely populated city in Japan and at the same time the most vulnerable of all the cities to be burned, according to the U.S. Strategic Bombing Survey conducted after the war. (This claim has been disputed by the Air Self Defense Force University.)

Metropolitan Osaka' s greater part was the slum district near the beach, which before the bombing was the most populous of the region: about 35,000 people per square mile in 1940.

In Japanese towns and cities, middle-class households are measured by approximately one bed per square yard. Because of the cultural difference, more people lived in Japanese slum districts than in American slums. People in Japanese slums lived in flimsy high-rise, easily burnable, primitive buildings on narrow streets with partitions instead of walls to separate the rooms.

In the Edo and Meiji eras, Osaka was famous for its show places, and Osaka's capitalist expansion led the country. In the beginning of the Showa era, before the war, Osaka was the leading mercantile city of Japan (called Smoke Town). From Osaka's central railroad station on a clear day you could see the clouds of smoke rising in the leaden sky from the steam locomotives in the station. The smoke from the factories rose day and night in great tall columns.

In the Meiji, Taisho, and Showa eras all sorts of big and small factories were built in Osaka. Sawmills crowded together, and people established home factories as well as giant companies. The population surged, slums spread, and general disorder increased. This gave Osaka a special flavor. The old city was consolidated—with fireproof buildings and wide streets, public parks, and empty spaces—to become the best-planned city in Japan.

And now, it was to be destroyed indiscriminately.

Along with Tokyo and Nagoya, Osaka had been bombed by Jimmy Doolittle's B-25 raiders in the spring of 1942, but the effect had been largely to prepare the Japanese for future bombings. Afterward the military authorities began to consider the possibilities of enemy bombing.

For the purposes of air defense, the war can be divided into two eras: B.D. and A.D.—Before Doolittle and After Doolittle.

Before Doolittle, Osaka had virtually no air defenses. After Doolittle, the Imperial General Staff decided to give air defense a new higher priority, and the number of antiaircraft guns around military installations was greatly increased. To Osaka, Nagoya, and Kobe city governments, this meant 110 new high-powered, high-altitude guns. However, it meant virtually nothing to civilians, for civil air defense was a function of the Home Ministry, and that ministry had decided that civilians had to provide their own defenses.

After Doolittle, the Japanese home islands *(hondo)* were indeed safe from air attack for a while, because the Americans had no bombers capable of attacking from the distant bases available to them. But in June 1944, the new B-29 Superfortresses began operations against Japan from western China with an attack on the Yawata Steel Works on Kyushu. The home islands barrier was breached.

Still, from their bases in western China (east China was in Japanese hands) the B-29s could hit only Manchuria and the northern tip of Kyushu. They did so several times, concentrating on the steel industry and doing considerable damage, particularly to facilities in Anshan, Manchuria. But most of Japan remained out of reach until the capture of the Marianas, when all Japan came into range.

Then in a series of midday raids the B-29s came to Tokyo, Nagoya, Osaka, and other cities. They hit Osaka first on November 27, 1944, in a daylight raid on the Musashi Factory No. 1 plant. Osaka Castle wasn't bombed, although bombs were scattered all over the countryside in what was a very spotty raid conducted mostly by radar. Fukuda Police Chief Yoshio Yoshizawa kept a diary in which he recorded that event.

On December 12, nine B-29s, soaring high in the sky, dropped bombs at leisure and then flew away, unmolested by Japanese fighter planes. Both *Asahi Shimbun* and *Mainichi Shimbun* newspapers reported on the bombing, according to Yoshizawa's diary.

Tokyo and Nagoya aircraft plants and military installations were hit, but Osaka was free of attacks until December 18. *Asahi Shimbun* reported:

> Today there was no bombing, but one sweep by a handful of B-29s on an observation mission showed how unready the city was for an air raid. In front of

the railroad station was an air-raid shelter where the toilets were plugged up with trash, So when the citizens and travelers dived in, they were greeted by unpleasant sights and a terrible stench. They shielded their faces and averted their eyes from what was definitely a civic embarrassment.

[Moreover,] enemy planes overhead could hear the radio report transmitted that the electric door outside failed so that sightseeing travelers on the exit of the enemy planes looked up; and had difficulty flooding into the street.

On the one hand it was an insignificant attack, on the other hand a serious reflection on the city government. It was an embarrassing situation for urban people.

The next day *Asahi Shimbun* reported:

At midnight enemy planes invaded the Osaka suburbs unobserved and dropped a few firebombs and flares, causing panicked flight.

To the bitter end the authorities concealed the names of the communities involved.

Osaka was left more or less alone until January 3, 1945. At about 2:30 in the afternoon the B-29s attacked with incendiaries; this was the first time that ordinary houses were burned. The city was attacked ten times in January and ten times in February. Still, altogether the damage was minimal.

Then came March.

Osaka, unlike Tokyo and Nagoya, had some warning about the beginning of the firebomb campaign. On March 4, a single U.S. B-29 flew over North Osaka and dropped hundreds of thousands of leaflets proclaiming the beginning of firebombing. But the warning was only an injunction to stay away from military installations. Readers of the leaflets might presume that if they did so they would be safe. There was no indication that civilian areas would be attacked.

A second B-29 appeared a few hours later and dropped more leaflets. These criticized the Japanese army *(Gunbatsu)* for starting the war and promised the destruction of the munitions industry. But they added that the Americans meant the Japanese people no harm, which, as was proved in the near future, was a barefaced lie.

An hour after the leaflet dropping an order went out as usual from the Osaka police to collect leaflets and deliver them to police headquarters. To read a leaflet or even to possess one was a crime in wartime Japan. Police were able to gather thousands of leaflets, but many thousands more were not turned in; many were picked up and passed hand to hand.

The decision to burn up Japan was made after those leaflets were dropped. On March 13 the B-29s of Tinian, Guam, and Saipan set out for their third big fire raid, and if anyone cared, the Americans could claim that the Japanese had been warned.

The production of Japanese war materials had begun with subcontractors and small home businesses, thus there was an element of truth in the U.S. military's claim that burning up Japan would have a direct effect on the supply of war materials. But, as everyone concerned knew, the real target of the bombings was Mrs. Suzuki and her children, the average Japanese.

The first fire raid on Osaka began the night of March 13 and ended in the early hours of March 14. It was obvious from the outset that the target areas were not confined to military installations, as the American leaflets had promised, but had been extended to housing and business offices. Even schools, public parks, and hospitals were not immune.

Forty years later residents recalled that the time between the alert and the all clear seemed to be an eternity. A single Pathfinder plane that carried 1,300 M-47 bombs led the B-29s. It provided aiming points, as had been the case in Tokyo and Nagoya. The B-29s came in from the west across Osaka Bay. As they first approached the searchlights, one or two Japanese fighter planes rose to attack but did not. The antiaircraft guns positioned to fire at planes coming in at high altitudes were completely confounded by the low-altitude approach.

Then the rain of firebombs began on the city suburbs and the sea of fire began to spread from the east. By 3:30 in the morning, the fire was in full force. The firestorm continued as 274 bombers dropped 1,733 tons of firebombs—burning up twenty-one square kilometers.

The assurance that civilians would be safe as long as they stayed away from military targets was a lie, as hundreds of families discovered. The B-29 attacks were concentrated on civilian targets.

Imajo-san was a distinguished citizen of Osaka and a member of the Harbor Board, which controlled the docks of this important port. The family lived in the Suiki district of Minato-ku, an area of subsidized houses clustered together. All their neighbors were young married couples, with only the wife at home usually, for the husband had gone off to war. The Imajo-san house was within walking distance of No. 2 Osaka Pier, which put it squarely inside the main target area for General LeMay's first fire raid on Osaka.

The family was in the garden that evening of March 13 when the air-raid sirens began to blow. Because they had been warned of the impending raid, they were wearing their air-raid costumes—baggy *monpei* trousers, loose shirts with long sleeves, standard air-raid jackets issued by the block authorities, and fireproof air-raid hoods. Daughter Kiyoko was the last to come out. She appeared just as the early warnings began at about 11 o'clock, when the B-29s passed over Cape Kamoda and then over Awaji Island. The sirens blew for four seconds, stopped for eight seconds, and then blew again for four seconds.

Down at the harbor the workers began streaming out of the factories, seeking shelter from the impending attack. The warning was repeated ten times.

Civil defense workers appeared on the streets in their distinctive uniforms, with megaphones to direct people. Near midnight the sirens began again, this time with an air of urgency—the planes were coming in over Osaka Bay. The men with the megaphones began to shout. The radio station at Kiisuido announced, "The enemy planes are on their way."

Osaka residents thought they were ready for the attack, They had been trained to fight fires. Neighbor would help neighbor, and they would beat out the fires with the flails supplied by the neighborhood associations.

The bombers arrived, their red exhaust flares clearly visible from below. The Imajo family watched as the planes came in over the bay, traveling toward the mouth of the Yasuhara River. Kiyoko looked out over the garden to the air-raid shelter the family had constructed. She thought about going down, but was fascinated by the droning of the B-29s as they came, and she stayed to watch the show. Suddenly bombs began to fall around the house, small six-pound firebombs that burned with a chemical intensity and could not be extinguished by water.

The antiaircraft guns opened fire but they were mostly ineffective; the planes were coming in too low. The civil defense officials watched as the bombs streamed down onto the roofs of Osaka, and wondered what to do.

Actually, there was nothing to be done, as the Imajo family discovered. The bombs hit the edge of the residential district and the fires spread until a firestorm began. Their young next door neighbor dived into the garden shelter, but the deafening sound transfixed Kiyoko. From the western sea a B-29 flew directly overhead and she saw a giant fuselage loom out of the darkness. This was followed by the appearance of many other planes, all of them marked with red wingtips. "What impertinence!" she thought. "The enemy is daring!" She became angry.

Kiyoko was a proper young Japanese woman, was knowledgeable about the military, and was brought up in the new *Bushido* tradition. Because of that she admired Japanese soldiers who sacrificed their lives for their nation, but she did not have any sympathy for the enemy dead. She hated the Americans and British. She gritted her teeth in silent rage at the thought of what the B-29s were doing.

The B-29s came on through the flames like waterfalls to the east, above Kiyoko's head. One block inland from the harbor was an allied POW camp. The prisoners expected the worst, but the firebombs began dropping about two blocks inland of the camp, then stopped for five miles in order to avoid the camp. They devastated the districts they attacked.

Takako Oshima was thirteen years old when Osaka was bombed, and lived with her parents and younger brother in Naniwa-ku, in south Osaka. Her father ran a shoe store. Her elder brother had enlisted in the army, her elder sister was married, and her younger sister, who was in the fifth grade, was among the elementary school students who had been evacuated to the country.

That night, March 13, she and her younger brother were sleeping in the family air-raid shelter, located in the family basement. It was very primitive, covered with very thin slabs of wood. A warning siren woke her up and she got dressed. Her father came to the shelter and told them, "There is something wrong tonight." Then she heard someone say, "They are dropping firebombs."

She jumped out of the shelter and saw that the western sky was burning like a sunset. And in the light of the fires, she saw a man bringing a hose. B-29s continued to fly over them, one after another.

She hid in the shelter and then went out to see what was going on. Her father told her, "Get out of here." She hesitated. "If we stay here, there is no solution. We will all die," he said.

The Oshima family left the shelter and began to run. Her mother stopped and said, "We must have some belongings." She took blankets from the closet and handed them to Takako. They went to leave the house, but her mother said, "Oops, I have forgotten something," and went back inside.

As soon as they stepped out, firebombs hit. Takako didn't remember what happened but she was assaulted by the noise and she fell down. She didn't know why, but Takako thought she was dead.

She got up and thought she stepped on a log, but knew there shouldn't have been a log there. Her feet were so very hot; when she looked down at her right foot, it was burning. In fact, almost her whole body was on fire.

She was facing the neighbor's house; their children were older and were boys. Why didn't they come and extinguish the fires from her body? she wondered. Then she jumped into the water cistern (nearly every house had a water cistern) and soaked herself up to her shoulders. That put out the fire.

She noticed that the skin of her right hand was hanging down in shreds, so she stuffed her hand back together. She began shouting and crying, "Mama,

Mama, Mama." Then two of the neighbor boys tapped her back to get her attention.

She thought, "We have to put out the fires," and she poured two buckets of water on the burning house. She was doing just what the fire drills said to do. "It's useless," her father told her.

Then she and her father went back to the water cistern and found her younger brother Saburo sitting there. Saburo was seven years old, and in the first grade. His face was swollen very badly, and he didn't have on a protective hood. In fact, he had no clothes on at all—nothing but a belt around his waist.

Takako and Saburo stared at each other without speaking. Saburo was so badly burned all over his body that Takako did not recognize him. He looked like a little pig that had been cooked. "Aren't you Saburo?" she asked him. He had changed so much.

Saburo stared at Takako and she stared back, unblinking. "It's a kind of game," Takato said. "The first one that laughs, loses." But it wasn't a game, not a game at all.

Father Oshima wanted to get away from the burning house but before they went they looked for Mother Oshima. They found her, inside the shelter, lying on her back under the stairs, dead of smoke inhalation. She had gone back into the house to get something and had become confused in the smoke. She had wandered into the shelter and fallen under the stairs. She had two burned out firebombs in her chest.

Takako knew that her mother had been inside the house. If she had told her father that her mother was inside the house, then her father would have left Takako and Saburo alone and tried to rescue their mother. "Then what would happen to me and Saburo?"

More than forty years after the war, Takako still felt guilty about this, feeling as though she had killed her mother.

The three other Oshimas hurried to the first aid center, where they were treated for their burns. However, Saburo's case was hopeless. More than 90 percent of his body was burned.

Saburo died the morning of March 16. As he was dying he muttered, "A soldier must always be loyal to the emperor!"

Toshie Kondo lived in Nishiku, a very old and traditional area of Osaka. Next door lived a master of *shamisen;* many geisha went there to have lessons. Her daughter Kumi was in the second year of senior high school. Her husband Junichi used to be an elementary school teacher, but had retired several years earlier. The couple ran a cram school for elementary students. The school was very popular; about a hundred children attended.

On March 13 at midnight, when the real air-raid warnings began, Junichi went to the nearby commercial school. He was a volunteer in the civil defense organization and his duty was to beat a gong when the air raid began, to beat in a rhythm saying, "The enemy bombers are coming to destroy us."

Toshie and Kumi and went into the shelter under the Natsume tree in their garden. They brought a first-aid kit and rucksack, which had water and emergency rations. They settled down to wait.

Their wait wasn't long. An M-69 Napalm bomb came down. Toshie drenched the bomb with water but it only seemed to burn more brightly. She smothered the bomb with a blanket. The fire ate the blanket. All her air-raid training was useless. Seizing her daughter's hand, Toshie ran out of the shelter.

They ran into the alley next to the narrow street; the alley was in flames. They went the other direction, and with an enormous effort broke a fence made of wood and ran away. When they looked back at their house it was in flames, and the second story was burning brightly. They prayed for their burning house.

Along the way Toshie and Kumi found a cistern full of water. Toshie soaked her fire hood and *hanten* in the water and then put them on, but they dried almost immediately. It was the same with her daughter's hood and jacket.

Toshie heard a loud, continuous noise: *Gong gonggggongongggg gongggg gong gong gong.* "Oh, my husband is banging," she said. "He must be on top of the school. Oh, no! He must get out of there! It is useless for him to keep banging. He must escape. Otherwise he is going to die."

But there was no way she could contact her husband, so she and Kumi ran in to the big street, an avenue where there were many shops. As they crossed toward a subway station, Toshie saw many people milling around the Daimaru department store. It had taken several firebombs and the roof and upper stories were on fire.

Mother and daughter entered the subway and stepped down into the staircase to flee from the fire. They sat down near the top to rest. Toshie's fire hood was now completely dry. She wondered where her scared feeling had gone.

Toward the bottom of the stairway she saw some light. "We may be saved," she thought. They began walking down the long staircase, hard going for two tired people. When they reached the bottom they saw a man with a red flag in front of the steel gate that led to the trains. "Please save this child," Toshie said to him.

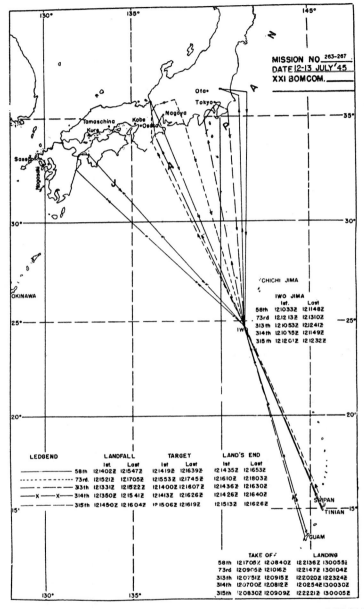

第8回中小都市空襲の航路図（1945年7月12—13日）。すべての航路は硫黄島を通過する。一作戦任務報告書より

Map showing distance from Marianas bases to Japanese target cities.

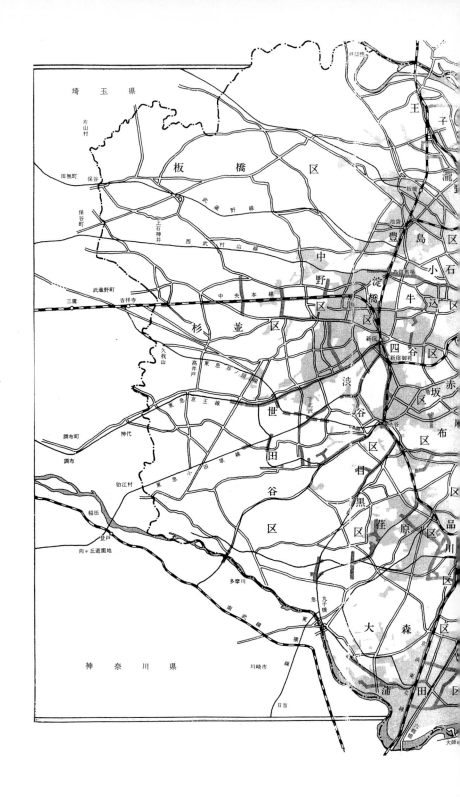

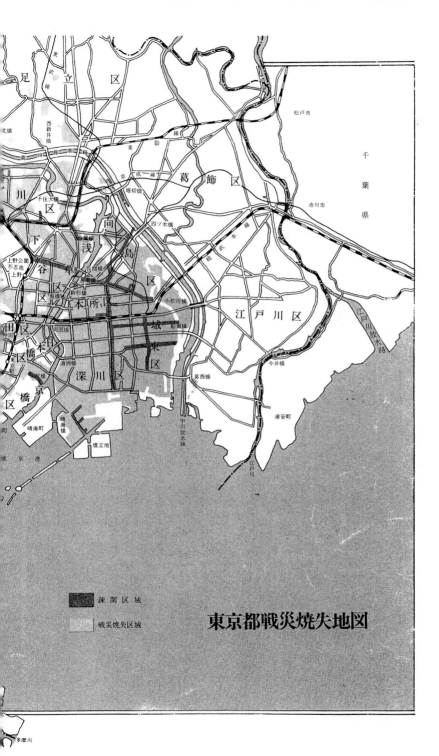

Map of Tokyo. Dark areas indicate extent of destruction from the firebombing

Tokyo after the firestorm of March 10, 1945. The Sumida River is in the center. Kyodo photo.

One tree was left standing. Kyodo photo.

Bodies taken from the Sumida River after the firestorm. The riverbanks were lined with many thousands of corpses, people who drowned while trying to escape the heat.

Firebombing refugees cluster in the wreckage of Tokyo on March 11, 1945.
Kyodo photo.

The burning of Nagoya castle, May 14, 1945. Chunichi Shimbun *photo.*

Nagoya after the firebombing. The city was destroyed, but the Mitsubishi aircraft factories remained intact. Chunichi Shimbun *photo.*

On March 17, 1945, 300 B-29s raided Kobe with firebombs. Except for the Tokyo raids, this was the most destructive attack: 8841 people died.

A schoolchild's drawing of the firebombing in Osaka.

In three great fire raids the B-29s destroyed 75 percent of downtown Osaka, as shown. The raids were on March 14, June 1, and August 14, 1945.

Hiroshima after the atomic bomb blast of August 6, 1945. Kyodo photo.

"Do you think it's all right if your daughter is saved and you are killed?" he asked. "Don't say that, both of you come in!"

About ten people stood near the subway entrance. The stationmaster shouted, "The Umeda area has not burned yet. Get on this train quickly!"

Toshie and her daughter went into the train. Other people rushed up and soon they were packed in like sardines, just like rush hour on Tokyo's Chiyoda line.

Toshie heard a young woman crying. "Oh my baby is gone!" The young woman gave a cry and felt her back. The harness for the baby was there, but no baby! "Oh, I've go to get off and go back," the frantic mother said. In her fear and hurry she must have been jostled and the baby thrown from her. "*Sumimasen.* Excuse me," she said as she tried to edge her way to the open door. Because the train was so crowded, she could not get through. The door closed and the train began to move. The train was running, and no one could help the mother.

The sky was dark when the train reached Umeda station. Toshie knew some people who lived in Yodogawaku, so she and Kumi went there. She still needed to find her husband, but there was nothing to be done that night.

The following day, she went back to her house and saw three firebombs in the shelter. They had finally burned out. On a wall inside the house were words scratched on the wall with charcoal: "You should go to Asahi ku." She knew her husband's cousin lived in Asahi ku. This rough sign must have been written by her husband, which meant he was safe. "Oh, Daddy is safe," she said to her daughter. "Come here, look at this sign. Your father is alive." They burst into tears of relief.

Lies, lies, lies! You could not believe anything the Americans said, the people of Osaka, Tokyo, and Nagoya realized after the raid on March 13.

By the middle of March 1945 Japan's four largest cities had each been attacked five times. Tokyo was hit hardest, on March 9, when 1,667 tons of bombs created a firestorm that burned 15.8 square miles. On March 12, 1,790 tons of firebombs burned 2.1 square miles in Nagoya. On March 17, Kobe was hit with 2,312 tons of bombs that burned 2.9 square miles. Two days later, on March 19, Nagoya was hit again, this time with 1,842 tons of bombs that burned 3 square miles. Altogether, Osaka was hit with 1,733 tons of bombs over 8.1 square miles.

In spite of the promises that only military targets would be attacked, shops, offices, department stores, banks, government offices, ma and pa stores, service establishments, and other businesses were destroyed in central Osaka. The downtown district was reduced to rubble.

The enemy planes scattered firebombs in densely populated areas—as many as ten bombs to a house. The only structures that did not burn were concrete buildings.

And the firebombing spread as General LeMay continued with his plan to burn up Japan

12

Kobe

On March 12, 1945, the day before the Osaka raid, one B-29 bombed Yokosuka, the big Japanese naval base, and the next day, March 13, two B-29s bombed the Nagasaki area. These obviously were aimed primarily at military intelligence targets with the added intent of keeping Imperial Headquarters guessing about the next move.

General LeMay was enormously pleased with the success of the Osaka raid. Aerial photos taken a few hours after the bombing showed that 8.1 square miles in the center of Osaka had been burned down, destroying 119 large factories and 200,000 houses.

It was an arsonist's dream come true, especially after the failure of the Nagoya raid, which LeMay blamed on his decision to lengthen the interval between bombs. The Osaka raid showed that the firebombers were back on track. LeMay wasn't overstating the situation when he said that, given enough bombs and enough bombers, he could burn up Japan.

The fourth raid was to be flown against Kobe, Japan's largest port and sixth-largest city. But more important, Kobe's population density was 100,000 per square mile. Flammability was high, particularly since the town, which had few rivers or canals flowing through it, depended on the water from three big reservoirs to fight fires. Ninety percent of the buildings were constructed of wood and paper and would burn like tinder. The date was March 16, two days after the Osaka raid.

To try to create another firestorm, like the one that had decimated Tokyo, LeMay selected four points along the long, narrow shore, where the city was heavily built up. LeMay ordered three hundred bombers to reach the targets at the same time.

The aircrews were beginning to object to having machine guns and ammunition jettisoned in favor of bombs. Japanese defenses in the last two raids had improved, and the fliers could expect more opposition over Kobe. So machine guns and gunners were restored to the bombers. The crews were informed that air–sea rescue operations had been improved with the addition of submarines and dumbo (amphibious) aircraft. Now if an aircrew was shot down over water, members could still be back at base in time for dinner.

On March 15, the newspapers were allowed to print reports of aid given to victims of the Tokyo fire raid of March 9. The Cabinet, in emergency session, ordered that Tokyo and other big cities be evacuated of all but essential defense workers. This meant the breakup of families, the ultimate destruction of the fabric of Japanese society. But there was no recourse for it and the people complied.

Kobe residents had noticed a few B-29s flying over their city in the past few days, and many of them had a gut feeling that they would be next on the attack list. On the night of March 16–17, their fears were realized. From the Marianas, 306 B-29s flew to Kobe and bombed. But because most of them bombed by radar from high altitude, the Japanese were aware only of the sixty-nine B-29s that came in at low altitude to bomb visually.

The Pathfinders came first, dropping M-76 five-hundred-pound bombs and napalm magnesium firebombs. (These bombs were designed for use against modern buildings. Magnesium kindled an extremely strong blaze that was impervious to water.)

The crews in the Pathfinders were responsible for target identification. The main force was to drop the same six-pound M-69 cluster bombs as were dropped on Osaka, but because of a bomb shortage would also use M-50 and M-17 cluster bombs. The M-17 was a four-pound thermite magnesium bomb, packed in five-hundred-pound clusters. Magnesium firebombing was very effective because Kobe had many shipyards and factories. The M-50 bomb was for use against large buildings.

Imperial General Headquarters had this to say about the Kobe raid:

> At about 4 o'clock on the morning of March 17, more than 60 B-29s attacked the Kobe area. Of these 20 were shot down. Almost all of the other planes suffered damage. The results of the bombing were not great damage.

Small wonder that the Japanese rarely believed Imperial Headquarters communiqués any more!

According to the U.S. military, three B-29s were lost in the raid, eleven were damaged, and 56 percent of Kobe was destroyed.

On March 21, *Asahi Shimbun* wrote:

> American aircraft ran away. When they came to Tokyo there were 130 B-29s, to Nagoya 130, Osaka 90, Kobe, 60. The figures are reducing because the Japanese Army attacks them and does them quite a lot of damage

In fact, the U.S. military had put into the air the largest number of B-29s yet mounted—331 planes. The difference between that figure and the one offered by *Asahi Shimbun* goes to show just how out of touch with reality even the Japanese press had become.

Kimiko Mikitani was walking along the main street of Misaki Honmachi district that night, toward her house on the north side of Dai Wada Bridge, when the air-raid sirens began to screech. People in the street began to panic, running this way and that, searching desperately for a place to hide from the U.S. bombers.

Kimiko, who was twenty-five years old, began to walk faster. Her house was not far away, only a few hundred yards on the other side of the bridge. On her back she carried her one-year-old son. She was pregnant with another child.

Her husband worked for the Mitsubishi aircraft company, which maintained a factory ten kilometers outside Kobe. The couple was looking forward to raising a family, although the war buzzed around their lives.

When Kimiko reached the far edge of the bridge she looked down. Below, on her right, she saw many people clustered underneath the bridge supports, some of them in the water. They had been told that the Dai Wada Bridge was as good as an air-raid shelter, were seeking protection there..

The B-29s came in one by one, flying low. Kimiko estimated their altitude at less than five hundred feet above the bridge. They began dropping their firebombs and suddenly the air was full of flying objects. The bombs fell on the bridge, in the river, on the shore, and as they exploded they emitted a bright white light and burned fiercely. These were the four-pound magnesium bombs. The ones that fell in the water burned faster than the others and gave off a dense smoke that hugged the water and crept around the bridge supports, blinding the people under the bridge.

The bridge's wooden supports began to burn, adding to the smoke and flames. The wind rose and blew hot and heavy. The fires made whirlwinds, one of which caught Kimiko's clothing and whirled her around so that she was facing back the way she had come on the bridge. Her air-raid turban caught fire, and her hair began to smoke and stink. She was most conscious of the stink. Her *monpei* caught fire and her arms and legs were burned.

The wind whirled her around again, and this time snatched the baby out of the harness on her back. She never saw him again. It was as if the God of War had swallowed him up, right there on the Dai Wada Bridge, in the middle of Kobe.

Even though Kimiko was in shock, she realized that she was burning and fell down on the bridge and rolled until the flames were out. Then she got up and began to run. She ran and ran, not knowing where she was running or why—just senseless motion.

By the time she had recovered her senses, she was wandering near the remains of her house, which had burned up into an unrecognizable mass of cinders and trash. She knew where she was only because, remarkably, a house across the street had not burned. It stood, a lonely sentinel, in the midst of the smoking rubble.

Meanwhile, the wooden bridge and its supports had burned and collapsed into the river. Five hundred people died below and on the Dai Wada Bridge that night—five hundred people and a baby swept from his mother's back into the water. The magnesium bombs continued to burn for many hours, lighting the night with their white-hot glow.

Kimiko realized that she was in need of first aid and went to a nearby hospital. She was admitted, examined by a nurse, and rejected. "You're not burned badly enough," she was told. "You should see some of these other people."

She wandered through the burned city, seeking assistance. Finally she came to an aid station where they treated her burns with salve, and gave her bandages for the worst of them.

The hurt in her body now matched the pain in her soul as she thought of the Fire Demon whisking away her first-born son. The only ones who would ever know Kimiko's intense pain were those thousands of other Japanese mothers who shared similar experiences.

Kimiko and her husband found each other the next day at a shelter in the center of Kobe. He had been working in the Mitsubishi factory. The factory hadn't been bombed, further evidence, some believed, that General LeMay's real target was the Japanese people.

Kimiko was eventually admitted to a hospital and stayed for several weeks, until her burns healed. She became extremely depressed over the death of her son and wondered if life was really worth living. But then her unborn baby began to kick, and that sign of life reminded her that there was more to life than war, death, and destruction. She had found something to live for.

In the summer of 1986 in Kobe, Kimiko was a happy, personable Japanese matron with no visible scars from her ordeal. But the firebombing of Kobe had left a lasting impression. She was deeply involved in the local efforts to bring relief to the local residents who had suffered most from the firebombing, a continual crusade that never seemed to get anywhere on the national level.

Shizue Nakamura lived on the beach in Nagata-ku, where she shared a house with four people. She was thirty-three years old, which would have made her nineteen at the time of the Manchurian takeover, and it seemed as though she had been standing in line for something ever since. The lines got even worse after Japan went to war with the United States in 1941; the last week had been the most difficult yet. On that day she had spent hours looking for a piece of cloth to make a *monpei* for her sister. She had gone to bed with the sun and was asleep when the bombers came and the air-raid sirens began to wail.

The house was dark until the fires from uptown began to flash in the glass door. She could tell that some part of Kobe was being burned up but she was exhausted and she did not care. She went back to the futon to get more sleep.

Then the air-raid siren began to blow across the street. She got up and dressed, and started for the Nagaraku elementary school, the nearest shelter. People everywhere were running to the school. Out past Cape Wada, she saw a ship sinking. For days afterward, the bloated corpses of the drowned washed up on shore.

The fires burned all night. Schools burned, as did hospitals and temples. The seven-hundred-year-old Yakusenji Temple, not far from the Dai Wada Bridge, burned to the ground. The dead of the city numbered 2,598, and the wounded numbered 8,558. The homeless numbered more than 650,000 and the homes of a million people were damaged. By official count, the raid left 236,000 "sufferers."

Yakusenji Temple was rebuilt shortly after the war. The temple priest, Satosho Goto, began a project to compile the names of all the dead killed in the Kobe air raids and became part of a committee to trace the history of the fire-bombing. This movement would become part of the great Japanese peace movement sparked by the atomic bombing of Hiroshima and Nagasaki.

The first fire raid on Kobe was very effective. When the bombers came to look the following day, they estimated that 56 percent of the city had burned up.

"That's all we need. There's no need to bomb Kobe again," General LeMay said. And he crossed Kobe off the target list.

13

Return to Nagoya

If General LeMay was concerned about the future, a statement that spring by General H. H. Arnold, chief of the U.S. Army Air Forces, should have comforted him. Arnold said he was looking forward to the day when General LeMay would have a thousand B-29s and could finish the burning of Japan in great style.

But the failure of the Nagoya raid still bothered LeMay. As previously noted, he blamed himself, stating:

> It seemed to me that we had been concentrating our detonations at Tokyo more tightly than we actually needed to, and by scattering bombs more widely, we could achieve the same results, but over a larger area. Thus, the bombs had been spaced to fall a hundred feet apart, and the result was that only two square miles of the city had been destroyed.

On March 18, 1945, General LeMay ordered another attack on Nagoya, to be carried out the next day. It would again be an incendiary raid, the only difference being that every third aircraft would carry two five-hundred-pound explosive bombs, to discourage firefighters, bring down power lines, break water mains, and cause confusion among those defending the city.

The XXI Bomber Command was scraping the bottom of its incendiary barrel, so nine types of firebombs would be used.

After four fire raids, Japan's air defenses should be much improved, the Americans believed. The Nagoya area hosted about two hundred heavy antiaircraft guns; ships in the harbor were also armed. The weaponry also included 170 automatic antiaircraft guns, effective at altitudes of about 2,500 meters. Those guns were made more effective by the fifty searchlights in Nagoya. The Japanese were very skilled in using searchlights to bring the B-29s into close observation and to blind the crews. To knock out the searchlights, the bombers would carry their lower gunners to fire on the ground targets. LeMay was hoping for cloud cover and smoke from the early fires.

As Domei's writer had predicted, the bastion of Iwo Jima had fallen to the United States. The U.S. bombers could soon have fighter escorts on their bombing missions. But the fields weren't ready yet for fighters. Once again, the B-29s would have to rely on speed and their own machine guns to face the 150 Japanese fighters that could be expected in the Nagoya area.

On the night of March 19, nearly three hundred B-29s descended on Nagoya to drop their deadly firebombs. People scurried out of the center of the city, prompted by civil defense officials with megaphones.

The Japanese called this night *yakan shodo sakusen,* "the night of scorched earth operations." After 1,860 tons of firebombs had fallen on the city, the newspaper *Chunichi Shimbun* reported, "the heart of Nagoya has been devoured." The good news was that only 828 people were killed and 228 were injured. Forty thousand houses were burned up.

Once again, damage to important military targets was put on the back burner. The destructive force was aimed at the heart of the city—houses, schools, hospitals, and shops. Several important aircraft factories were located in Kagamigahara, north of the city. The bombers ignored them. Part of the Toyo Cotton Mill was burned down, as was the Yamada airplane engine works, but companies just happened to be surrounded by shops and houses. The searchlights were not as much of a problem as the Americans had feared. Several bombardiers reported that they had been so blinded as they released their bombs that they didn't know if they had hit a target. High winds created a minor firestorm. The next morning, as the planes flew back to the Marianas, the streets of Nagoya were littered with burned out streetcars, trucks, carts, wagons, and bicycles.

Of the B-29s that attacked that night, one was hit by antiaircraft fire and its crew had to ditch the plane on the way home. They were all rescued.

The attackers were met by 192 Japanese fighters, but only thirty-seven pressed home an attack and only one fighter managed to damage a bomber. Another Japanese fighter tried to ram a bomber but failed.

Four Japanese fighters that jumped a straggling B-29 thirty miles west of Tori Shima conducted the most spectacular defense counterattack. The four made twelve coordinated attacks on the bomber, one plane using its landing lights to illuminate the plane for the others. But they did not down the B-29.

When the results were in, General LeMay announced that in five raids his bombers had destroyed thirty-five square miles of Japanese industrial cities.

But that was not the end of it. On March 24 the B-29s attacked Nagoya again. At 10:44 that night, Radio Tokyo gave its early warning:

It is suspected that large formations of a large type enemy plane have headed toward Nagoya and should arrive between 11:30 and midnight.

Although these instructions are frequently given, have every possible container filled with water, keep things inside and outside your house in order, and have everything prepared so that you will be able to fight without anxiety.

As soon as the movements of the enemy planes become clear they will be announced promptly, hence, rest yourselves and be calm just before dashing out to fight.

Things remained calm for about two minutes. Then Radio Tokyo was on the air again. The enemy planes were indeed heading for Nagoya. At 11:08 the radio announced an air-raid warning for the Tokaido area, which extended from Tokyo to Nagoya.

At 11:47, the announcer asked if the public was ready for the battle. "Let us fight tonight again. Are you sure there are no obstacles in your path?" He asked the civil defense teams, "Are you sure all your men are at their stations?"

First it was four, then it was more planes that were heading for Nagoya. At 12:15 Radio Tokyo announced that the U.S. planes would fly over Nagoya from several different directions. "But Japanese planes, too, are heading for Nagoya to intercept the enemy."

At 12:56 the announcer was on the air again: "Number one has penetrated Nagoya. Number two will soon penetrate Nagoya. Number three is heading over the water north of Tsu." And at 1:11: "The enemy planes are dropping incendiaries and explosives. Be sure to wait in case of the explosives, for them to go off, but dash in to put out the incendiary fires."

After two raids that month, Nagoya residents were not expecting another, and many had chosen this lovely evening to go for a walk in the open area around the industrial district. Sensako Sugiyama was one of them. She was caught by a firebomb and her *monpei* and air-raid turban were set afire. She dropped to the ground and rolled over and over to extinguish the flames, but her arms, hands, and face were badly burned.

At 1:21 the radio announced, "Our intercepting units are fighting gallantly. One enemy plane has been shot down. Some people must have seen the plane go down with black smoke streaming behind it."

At 1:26: "The fight against incendiary bombs is decided in the first five minutes. Please extinguish fires before they spread." The announcements continued through the early morning: 1:30, "Taking out your household goods is important"; 1:33, "You must not hesitate to destroy houses in the vicinity of fires"; 2:06, "Our air defense units have shot down another plane"; and, finally, 2:31, "The air raid warning is hereby lifted from the Tokaido area."

That night, according to Japanese reports, 130 B-29s hit the city with 1,540 tons of firebombs, killing 1,716 people, injuring 770, and burning 7,600 houses. The real tragedy of the bombing was the burning of an elementary school that had been turned into a public shelter. Several hundred women and children were broiled, trapped inside with no chance to escape. However, work at the Mitsubishi plants continued, because those buildings had not been primary bombing targets.

The B-29s came to Nagoya again on March 30 and April 6. The central railroad station was burned during the April 6 raid. More people were killed, more houses incinerated. But by this time Nagoya was almost completely numbed to the bombing. It was not the size but the frequency of the raids. People could not remember back when they had not been bombed with fire day after day.

Much has been made of the negative effect of the firebombings on Japanese home morale. However, Japan's citizens were resigned to the war, and possibly to the death of many. To be sure, production at the Mitsubishi plants fell because many workers left their posts when the air-raid sirens went off so they could be with their families. But that didn't mean that they expected Japan to surrender. Like soldiers digging their caves on the Kyushu shore, the civilians waited for the worst. When the Imperial government announced Japan's surrender August 15, the nation went into deep shock. Japan had expected a U.S. invasion and was prepared to fight to the death. "*Shikata ganai!* There is nothing to be done.*"

By the end of March 1945, Sensako Sugiyama had decided that Japan had lost the war, but she did not expect the government to surrender. She was not privy to the thoughts of Emperor Hirohito, who had concluded the same, but was determined to do something to save his people.

14

Tokyo's Troubles

On April 14, 330 B-29s bombed Tokyo; on April 15, 109 B-29s bombed the city. The killed and wounded were a handful compared with the more than 100,000 killed in the holocaust of March 9. The casualties totaled 6,795 on April 14 and 2,171 the next day, according to an Imperial Capital Defense Headquarters report. However, on March 9 in Kototoi Bashi alone at least 5,000 people were believed to have been killed.

Tokyo citizens were becoming very skilful at running away. Until March 9, Tokyo residents were told not to flee if they saw a fire. They were told to pull up their socks and wade in like samurai should. "To extinguish firebombs is part of the war," the Home Ministry announced. And indeed, many risked their lives to put out the fires.

Actually, Tokyo had a long history of fires and arson, dating back to the Tokugawa shogunate, when the capital was called Edo. "The Flowers of Edo," as Tokyo's fires were then known, were famous throughout Japan. Because of that, fire drills became the rule in Tokyo, and the practice spread to the rest of the country.

How, then, could so many errors have occurred?

The experience of March 9 offered a vivid explanation as to how wrong the official instructions were. The incendiary bomb burned with an intense flame, and when several thousand of them were dropped in a small area it was like a deadly rain. At the same time, fire fighting—the bucket brigades and other primitive methods used when the fire mains failed—was futile. Nevertheless, the samurai tradition prevailed and Tokyo citizens tried their best.

After the fiasco on March 9, Tokyo residents knew that fighting the incendiary bombs would be useless. Instead, they should respond to their gut feeling and take shelter.

Eventually, many people began to question the war and the weeping, pain, and suffering it brought. They also began to read the leaflets dropped by U.S. planes, an act that could lead to an arrest.

A schism began to develop between the people and their leaders. The people began to talk about a quick end to the war, but the leadership was still talking about the "final decisive homeland battle."

General LeMay was just getting started in his campaign to burn up Japan. A month later, May 24 and 25, he ordered even bigger raids.

On May 24, 525 planes raided; the following day, 470 planes attacked what was left of Tokyo. The two raids destroyed twenty-two square miles. By now, 50.8 percent, or fifty-six square miles, of Tokyo had been burned. The Americans called this "the heart of Tokyo raid," and that it was. Because the government buildings around the Diet and the Imperial Palace were mostly modern, the M-76, the five-hundred-pound incendiary bomb, was used, as well as the lighter bombs meant for small structures. Two city blocks of the Ginza shopping district were wiped out in those raids. U.S. bombers also attacked and burned the Nagoya industrial belt, and shopping and residential areas.

But the most significant action of those two days was on May 25, when General LeMay's fliers attacked the Imperial Palace. The palace area had been declared an "open city" and was *never* to be bombed—a promise made by U.S. President Franklin D. Roosevelt. The reason: the United States hadn't yet determined if Emperor Hirohito was responsible for the war, and there was the possibility that he would be charged with war crimes.

But it appeared that General LeMay's fliers respected neither persons nor promises. The U.S. high command claimed later that the palace bombing was accidental, that only the homes of the prime minister and other Japanese leaders had been targeted. Further:

> Almost all bombardiers excepted the Imperial Palace aiming point but in the night bombing they failed to verify accuracy and so the palace, segregated from the government by its distinctive wide moat, was bombed by at least one plane.

However, one of the pilots on that raid claimed credit for the "accident." Charges were never made against the pilot, nor was the bombing investigated.

The Imperial Palace was established in the Tokugawa era as Edo Castle. During its history, the castle suffered nine fires. Emperor Meiji moved to Tokyo on October 23, 1868, and changed the name of Edo Castle to Tokyo Castle. After his marriage in 1869, he renamed it yet again to Imperial Castle.

Fire hit the palace area again in 1874. A temporary Imperial Palace was established in Akasaka Rikyu while the new permanent palace was being constructed within a moat area. Sixteen years later, the emperor was able to return, and changed the name to Kyujo. The name remains today.

As Japan entered World War II, the emperor and empress had an air-raid shelter built under the Fukiage Gyoen in 1941 (its secret name was Fukiage Gobunko). The shelter was three stories deep, with a ground floor, where the imperial family and their entourage could live; a service level with air conditioning and ventilation equipment; and a deep shelter with living accommodations, servants quarters, and a large meeting room. Emperor Hirohito and the empress moved into the shelter in 1943, when it became obvious that Tokyo would be bombed.

On May 25, Hiroshi Shimamura, minister of State, was in the underground air-raid shelter at the home of Kantaro Suzuki, Japan's prime minister. After the bombing started it was not long before the prime minister's house began to burn, along with the homes of many other officials. Smoke came into the prime minister's shelter, where many executives had taken refuge.

At about 3 o'clock in the morning, the chief of staff brought about ten people into the shelter. After a while many of them climbed up to the roof and looked out. Shimamura joined them. Then he saw a huge pillar of flame rising above the bushes that concealed the Imperial Palace. "This scene was beyond description," Shimamura said.

He bowed low three times to the Imperial presence, and went down.

Kazuko Ochi's apartment was burned during the raid of May 25. That day, the air raid began at 9 o'clock at night, Kazuko told writer Motoyuki Manabe in 1976, when Manabe was writing his book. But official records report that the air-raid warnings began at 10:22. The air defense command's central headquarters was in the Tokyo Metropolitan Police Board, and their records are very fuzzy. For instance, official records aren't clear as to how many people were killed in the two raids. (The same suspicion applies to the overall figures of the Tokyo air raid of March 9. Official records record 88,000 as killed but the number for that one raid may have been as high as 150,000. For this book, the figure of 130,000 is used.) Therefore, while writing his book, Manabe relied on Kazuko's version.

And so on May 25, Kazuko experienced her first big air raid. She lived in Bunkyo-ku where only a few stray bombs had dropped before, but this air raid burned many historic buildings, including a very famous temple called Denzuin in Koishikawa. Kazuko's apartment was near the Denzuin.

When the air raid began, Kazuko and the other people living in her building rushed into the shelter in the garden. Once inside the shelter, one of them said, "No way. Let's get out of here," and he jumped out of the shelter. This

man had already lived through three air raids, so he had a very sharp gut reaction to the impending danger.

Kazuko shared that sense of danger. The air raid "was so bad and it got so
hot inside the shelter that I was afraid that all of us would be roasted," she
recalled. So Kazuko followed him out of the shelter and ran up a steep hill to
the famous Red Gate of Tokyo University—a pretty rough climb under any
conditions—up to Kikuzaka in Hongo from Hatsunecho in Koishikawa. A
friend, Michiko Murata, who lived in the same apartment building, ran with
her. By this time it was already midnight.

Once the two friends reached the Red Gate they didn't know where to go.
They looked around and noticed a little temple nearby. It was bare and had
no facilities. It would be like camping in the open. "This evening we must
stay here," Kazuko said to her friend.

"It can't be helped, can it?" Michiko said.

"This place will be good, because it won't be cold," Kazuko said. The two
settled into the veranda for the night, and after a little while began to doze.

Suddenly they woke up. The area was filled with light.

"Dawn has come," Kazuko said. "Let's go back and look at the apartment."
Michiko nodded her agreement and stood up.

Perhaps the apartment had not been completely destroyed, they thought. The
fire seemed to have disappeared. They had put night supplies and many cooking utensils in the air-raid shelter. If the fire had not destroyed these things
perhaps they could save them. Kazuko also wanted to see how the other ten-
ants survived the night.

Kazuko and Michiko began to walk, slowly retracing their steps back to
their apartment building. Along the way they found a homemade bed and made
plans to return for it.

As they walked closer to their apartment building, they could see that it had
not burned up. In fact, it was the only building in the area that had not been
destroyed, although one part had collapsed and it was filled with smoke inside. As soon as Kazuko entered the building, she knew her room had burned.
Within a moment Kazuko fainted from the smoke. There, in the closed space
of the room, the smoke level was high, the oxygen scanty.

When she came to, she was on a stretcher in the garden. Michiko was looking down at her. "Don't do such silly things. You startled me. I thought you
were dead," Michiko said.

"Somebody rescued me," Kazuko said.

"Somebody rescued you. You are on that stretcher thanks to Kinoshita-san.
He brought the stretcher," Michiko said.

Kazuko looked up at a tall broad-shouldered young man who was smiling down at her. Kazuko knew him. They all lived in the same building. His full name was Kenji Kinoshita. When Michiko had shouted for help, he had brought the stretcher inside the smoke-filled room and rescued Kazuko.

"It was a foolish thing to do" Kazuko said to him. "I accept with thanks your saving me. Thank you very much. Surprisingly I feel fine. My head is already clear." As she was talking, Kazuko got up.

Hamada, a young person who also lived in the apartment building, walked up to them and said, "Here it is, here it is! Michiko." He was carrying a big flower-patterned futon.

"Oh there it is," Michiko said. "What happened to the futon? It was mine, I must have put it in the air-raid shelter."

"I was looking for things at the Thieves' Market," Hamada said. "I discovered this and managed to buy it back."

"Thieves' Market? What do you mean?" Michiko asked.

The market was where thieves would sell items that they stole from houses and apartments that were emptied during the air raids. It was a capital offense at that time to loot during an air raid but the police did not have the strength to enforce the laws, so that law went unheeded.

Here is what happened to Michiko's futon:

After the firestorm had passed, Kinoshita returned to the air-raid shelter in the darkness, and found a stranger taking things. He shouted at the man to stop, but the man ran away.

Kinoshita knew that something was missing from the shelter, but he couldn't figure out what.

Later Hamada, who had a little of the Yakuza (gangster) in him, told him about the Thieves' Market. They went there to look for the missing items, and found Michiko's futon.

"I know whose that is," Hamada said.

"Sez you," said the Yakuza who was running the place. "Prove it."

"That futon came out of the shelter at my apartment house. It belongs to a girl I know. Hand it over."

"The hell I will," the Yakuza said.

"Then I'll take it," Hamada said, grabbing the futon.

The Yakuza grabbed it back and hit Hamada in the nose. Hamada hit him and they began scuffling and pummeling each other. Finally Hamada knocked the Yakuza down, threw money at him, and walked off with the futon.

15

The Road to Hiroshima

During April and May, B-29s would fly above Osaka but not bomb, and people began to feel more secure. But everyone knew that the Americans had invaded Okinawa so the soldiers were supposed to be preparing to fight on the beaches of the home islands. According to secret documents, many people from Osaka and Wakayama were digging caves at Kiisusido fortress to make last-ditch fortifications.

Some of the excavators were junior high school students from Osaka who were boarded on a train and not told where they were going. They slept on the floor of an elementary school or on the ground at a sake distillery and were always hungry but that made no difference. The excavators, young and old, were expected to dig into the rock without tools.

On May 9, just after midnight, a single B-29 was shot down over Takaida. The almost complete fuselage fell in the center of Takaida, Higashi San Chome's neighboring Shinkita, about 1.5 kilometers from Tatezucho Nakano. Bits of wreckage were scattered in the fields in a dozen places. One engine with a propeller smashed into houses, killing two and injuring four. The ten crewmen were killed.

On May 10, *Mainichi* newspaper reported: "Japanese weapons get B-29 over Osaka as people had long wished." When people looked at the headlines they got excited; the only other time they had read about a B-29 being shot down was on March 14. But that was a time of great chaos and there were no witnesses.

This time there were many witnesses. At dawn, many gawkers came to Takaida. Some them took revenge on the American crewmen's bodies, kicking and slapping them. The B-29 had much fuel aboard so there was a big fire on the ground.

And the air raids continued. Air raids were repeated on Osaka in the daytime on June 1, 7, and 15. Kobe was hit on May 5 and 9 (although General LeMay had made much of taking Kobe off the list of targets after the first raid).

Girls and boys were forced to work in the factories, so there were no school commencement ceremonies, no spring, summer, or winter vacations. On June 1 in Osaka, forty schoolgirls were working in the port office. They wore their school uniforms and very shabby shoes; some wore *geta*, or rubber-soled sandals. Shoes were in short supply, and so were rationed. That day the Osaka area was attacked by more than four hundred B-29s, accompanied by P-51 fighter planes. After the B-29s bombed, the P-51 fighters strafed the Osaka Harbor area.

Taneko Fujikura recalled that she and others crouched under railroad vans to escape the strafing. Some of the girls were saying Buddhist prayers. Some of them were calling each other's names and hugging them to make sure they were alive. Luckily the P-51s were not very accurate and all the girls were safe.

While Taneko was hiding she saw a soldier with burns all over his body. His uniform was burned off, and his skin was hanging down from his chest and shoulders like moss from a banyan tree. He was swaying back and forth like a drunk. She worried about him.

The girls were supposed to have in their bags burn medicine, dried beans, and yellow powder medicine to stop bleeding. Taneko went to help the man but a female teacher shook her head, signaling that Taneko should not go near him. "There is no hope of saving him," Taneko recalled, so she backed away. The man wandered away from sight.

The girls came out from under the railroad cars and jumped into Osaka Harbor, in their school uniforms. They soaked their fire hoods in the water and put them on again but they dried almost immediately in the hot summer air. One of the schoolboys dropped his hat into the water and drowned trying to retrieve it, Another boy tried to rescue him but he, too, was drowned. The schoolgirls watched the boys and laughed. They did not realize what they were seeing. Any sense of reality had completely disappeared.

Akiko Watanabe's father was killed in the P-51 strafing. Many people had crowded into a cave near the bridge, but the cave was too small and about fifteen people were forced to stand in the cave's opening.

When the P-51 came down, machine guns spitting, the people fell like logs. Akiko's mother was one of them; she was pushing a baby stroller when an explosive bullet hit her in the hip. She was disemboweled, her intestines scattered in pieces. There were no injuries on her upper torso, so she looked as if she were sleeping peacefully, but she was dead. In the inside pocket of her jacket she had a flashlight. In the stroller were a kettle and pans for cooking.

Seventeen-year-old Kiyoko Imajo witnessed a P-51 machine gunning that day. She had survived the first firebombing of Osaka (the night she became so angry with the Americans that she gritted her teeth in rage). She was studying in a seminary to become a teacher, but she had this day off and so was at home.

When the air raid began she and her mother, Sadako, were in the shelter cave of their home. A dud bomb the size of an oxygen cylinder came through the roof and into their kitchen. That's how they knew the firebombing had started. They evacuated the house and ran to the Hiyori Bridge, crossed over Kaigan Dori to the railroad track, and reached the dock. The P-51s came down as they neared the Kaigan Dori and strafed. Three P-51s came down low and flew like acrobats, diving, rolling over, and zooming up. They saw a factory girl get shot in the head and die and a horse get hit in the leg; he fell and was struggling on the ground.

Kiyoko Imajo heard ripping noises and counted fifteen bullet holes in the bridge's concrete balustrade. The P-51s had narrowly missed her.

Yoshiko Yamano, twenty years old, was a typist at a big company office in Honcho 12 chome, in the center of Osaka. The office building had burned down during the great air raid in March, so the company had moved. When Yoshiko arrived at the office that morning, she heard the air-raid siren and evacuated with her coworkers.

Most company employees went to the basement. Yoshiko went outside, through the company gate, and started for the office of a friend whom she had agreed to meet. She was walking up the road when she heard the sound of low-flying airplanes, and looking up she saw that they were U.S. P-51 fighters that were getting ready to strafe.

Yoshiko was scared and started to run. She passed by the branch office of the Bank of Japan. She could hear the noise of the P-51s firing from her left.

She felt a shock in her right ear and then heard nothing. She thought perhaps that the noise had broken her eardrum. She looked up; a low black airplane flashed by in an instant, and she ran and ran, crossed the bridge, then went in to the Dokima Company building. The company employees were in the basement. Yoshiko called her friend's name and she replied, "Here."

Suddenly the firebombs began dropping like rain. The building shook and the basement filled up with smoke and flames. "Let's get out of here. It is very dangerous," somebody said.

Yoshiko and her friend left the basement and headed for Yoshiko's house. "Get down!" said a voice. "Get down!" She dropped flat on the ground. The road ahead suddenly exploded in fire and smoke.

A P-51 flashed by. Yoshiko's body went rigid and she thought her breathing had stopped. She sensed the big shadow of a fighter aircraft over her. Then in a rush it was gone and the air was empty and silent.

The B-29s disappeared, and Osaka began to pick up the pieces.

The B-29s returned June 5 to the Hanshin area, which meant Osaka and Kobe.

Takeo Ikuma lived in the Fukiai district, on the west side of Kobe. From their house on the hillside, his family had an excellent view. And from the second story veranda Takeo could see the bombers as they came in. The bombers arrived in broad daylight on this hot summer day, and at first the smoke from the attack hung in the air, rising lazily. Then the wind rose and the fires began to spread.

Takeo could see the air raid very clearly. He saw a Japanese fighter pilot crash into a B-29, and saw the parachutes stringing out behind the collapsing bomber. The planes were flying high, which they had been doing recently. They looked like great lazy birds as they drifted along and dropped their deadly pellets. Half an hour after the raid began, Takeo's aging father and his sisters moved out of the house and walked to the shelter behind the hill, while Takeo remained to fight the firebombs if they came his way. Takeo was expecting disaster; he had a hunch that his family's house would not escape bombing today.

The black smoke began to move toward Takeo's house. Most of the people in this area had already fled, although by law they were supposed to stay and protect their houses. At first Takeo thought the planes were dropping M-69s. He was wrong. The planes were dropping M-50 magnesium bombs, the kind that water would not douse.

Several bombs fell on Takeo's house, and he rushed to grab one of the many buckets of water that he had assembled to fight fires. He threw water on one of the bombs, but all it did was make the bomb sputter and burn more brightly. Takeo realized then that he couldn't stop the fire, and that he had to escape while there was time. By then, the fire surrounded his house.

The best escape route now seemed to be along the electric railway line, where the embankment was relatively free of buildings. He figured there would be fewer flames and set out along that route. But to reach the train line, he had to get through the streets and past the burning houses.

As he made his escape, he passed many people who were fleeing to the mountains, carrying babies on their backs, or suitcases, bags, boxes or futons.

Some loads seemed so heavy he wondered if the people would make it to safety. A number of policemen were on the embankment, trying to control the crowds that were streaming from the city. Firefighters were trying desperately but vainly to stem the blazes. Through the smoke Takeo heard cries of anguish and fear as people tried to get help for themselves or a loved one. The people moved like a great wave, washing away from the yellow fires.

Takeo felt dull pain in his hands and looked down. Both hands were burned from his efforts to put out the fire at his house, but one of them had turned a strange white color. He came to a large barrel of water and plunged his hand in. The surface was covered with an oily scum, which meant he could not drink it, so he gave the barrel a kick and went on.

Everywhere he saw people searching for friends and relatives, calling out names, walking along with vacant eyes. And he began to see the debris of war, futons cast aside by people who found them too burdensome to carry, pots, pans, bundles of clothing, and all the tools of civilization that had become unimportant in the rush to get away from the flames.

He reached the edge of the hills at Noda Machinaga. All the houses were abandoned. He found a trickle of water and cooled his aching hand. The trickle went down the hill, to the Ikuta River, but the river area was being bombed now. He figured the place to go was the upland area ahead, which the bombers were bypassing. There were not enough houses on the hills.

Takeo also wanted to check on his family in the shelter. But to do that he would have to cross a sea of fire. The place to go was the mountain. But he was so tired. Wearily, he forced his legs to move on.

When he reached the highland and looked down, he saw that his part of Kobe had really taken a beating. In fact, he could see that the town had burned, from Fukiai to Ikuta. The green trees were burning, and beyond them the houses were still afire. He looked across at Katano Kijo landing, which had been a designated shelter. It was almost totally burned up, along with the people who had taken refuge there.

He had come as far as he need. The planes were leaving and the fires were dying out. He sat down and put his back against a building's stone wall. He was furious about the beating his city had taken from the enemy—indignant, resentful, and defeated; crushed; wiped out. It was, he said to himself, the end of his world.

Takeo suddenly remembered his father and sisters, and decided to go to the shelter to find them. As he got up, he saw that the wall he had been leaning on was stained with his own blood. He was beginning to feel a pain in his back, but couldn't remember how he had been wounded. He saw a group of people on the road and stopped them. One man looked at his back.

"Go to an aid station" the man said. "That wound on your back looks pretty awful. You must have a doctor look at it." The man turned away and walked after his friends. Takeo could hear the laughing and chattering as they wandered along the road.

Takeo walked back down to the plain, where it seemed that everyone in Kobe had now congregated, calling out names, searching for family. The people were covered with dust, dirt, and soot. The Fukiai district had indeed gone up in smoke.

He was feeling very weak now and knew it was from loss of blood. He finally found an aid station and a doctor. The doctor took one look at his white face and gave him a spoonful of sugar. It seemed to revive him. After looking at his back, the doctor told him that the wound had been caused by a bomb fragment, and that he had seen scores of them this day. He told Takeo to lie down. The nurses put something on his wound and bandaged it but that was all they could do. They had virtually no medical equipment.

Takeo rested for a while and then set out again on his search. He found his family at the shelter on the other side of the hill, safe and unhurt. Takeo and his family went back to their house—or where their house had been. There was nothing left but a heap of ash and twisted metal.

The authorities gave them food and supplies for five days. They gave the family bedding and a canvas tarpaulin. Takeo, his father, and sisters found a pleasant grove that had escaped the fire, on a hillside next to a stone wall, and set up camp there. They remained there for two days, numbly aware that everything in Kobe was gone. A school and three public buildings had been set aside as morgues. Every day people arrived, searching for their loved ones and too often finding them.

The heat from the structure fires remained for three days. Finally Takeo and his family realized that they were still alive, and must do something for themselves. Everyone they knew was dead or missing. Since there was no reason to remain in Kobe, they decided to leave and go to where Takeo's father's relatives lived.

And so, on the fifth day after the raid that burned them out, Takeo and his family went to the central railroad station in Kobe and took a train that would take them to a place of refuge and a new life.

They got on the train for Hiroshima.

16

Adventures of a Soldier

On March 22, 1945, the Americans occupied Ioto. In the last ten days of April the U.S. Army's hand fell on Okinawa. Thus it was coming already, as someone prophesied: Japan's defeat.

Japan's military authorities were still saying that the decisive battle of the homeland (100 million Kamikazes) would turn the tide. The military establishment refused to accept the idea of defeat and the resulting surrender. Their hearts were set on the plan of no surrender, even though most civilians wanted to end the war.

That thought struck Manabe, the magazine editor, as once again a red card, a draft notice, was delivered to him in Tokyo. At that time conditions were growing desperate, and many soldiers who had served before were being drafted again. Those who did not respond to a draft notice could be shot. Without delay he went to see the company president. "I have to go to the army again," he said. "I'm sorry. With this bombing and all, the magazine business is getting worse and worse. But please make sure everything is all right here."

"So you are waiting to become a soldier," the president said. "Well, well, That's tough. Everything's tough these days . . . However, don't worry about the magazine. Everything will be all right. Go ahead and enlist in the army. We don't know when this company building will be destroyed by the air raids but as long as the company remains here your salary will be paid to your family."

What could one say to that? Manabe had nothing to say.

Paper for magazines was rationed then. The army and navy took virtually all paper products, so civilians and businesses got almost nothing. No paper, no press run—the company would be out of business very soon. "The magazines are really going to hell," Manabe thought.

"Every time we had an air raid, we lost not only human lives but buildings, enterprises, and industries," he said. "We were forced to shut down. Lack of materials, nonfunctioning—production in limbo —this must happen to publishing, banking, industry, merchants, farmers. There is no exception . . .

"After I enlisted in the army this second time," Manabe said, "I was living in a lodge on the Pacific ocean in Kochi Province, on the island of Shikoku. Soldiers usually live in barracks. Truly in Manchuria I did. But in Kochi there were very few barracks, particularly on the narrow coastal plain that butts up against the mountains. This lodge I lived in was little more than a wood hut.

"Here we soldiers didn't have any drills. We were told we were waiting for the 'decisive battle' that our superiors had promised us to stop the Americans from landing on the sacred soil of Japan," Manabe recalled.

"By summer the American Army had already taken Okinawa and the soldiers. In Kochi we knew we didn't have time to lose. The decisive battle would be coming very soon.

"We had our orders from the military. When the Americans land, you will stay and fight to the death. Meanwhile you will dig. So we dug, and dug, and dug. This was no ordinary digging, not like digging in a garden. It was more like mining, and the only tools we had were picks and shovels. We were digging caves, into which we would retreat ultimately to fight the decisive battle, taking so many of the enemy with us to hell that they would back off from their invasion."

He continued: "We were to fight to the last man, but we did not have anything with which to fight. The Japanese Army at home did not have any weapons. The Army didn't have any uniforms to spare; not even shoes; so we wore *waraji* —sandals made of straw. A soldier had to be able to make his own *waraji*. If he didn't have any skills he had to go barefoot.

"Soldiers' apparel in those days was not fashionable. Soldiers didn't care about fashion. The important thing was the ability to fight again." But they had no weapons, no machine guns, no rifles, no bayonets.

"Our Army officers told us to fight to the end but they did not give us soldiers any weapons or tell us how to fight without weapons." When Manabe thought about this he concluded it was ridiculous; there was no way they could fight. But *shikata ganai!* There is nothing to be done.

"We were soldiers and we were not allowed to complain about anything, not allowed to question anything. Just take action. Just do what we were told to do. We were told to dig and so we dug. We dug without any hesitation and stayed in the huts. We worked with pick and shovel—worked with pick and shovel from early morning until late at night. That was all.

"Suddenly one day, I was told something unexpected," Manabe said. "When I was looking at the train timetable, I found that no trains stopped at Imabari station. Imabari City in Ehime Province, next to Kochi, had a population of sixty thousand people; it was the third biggest city in Ehime. But it was no longer listed on the timetable. No time schedule, but small dots in the lineup only . . ."

He continued: "I wondered why this was. Wondered why the third largest city in the province had no train service. It sounded ridiculous . . . I asked a friend why this was so. 'Hey, look at the timetable—no Imabari Station any more. How come?'

"The other guy said, 'Wow! No Imabari Station. No Imabari Station? But the station is there. All the trains pass by Imabari Station.'

"A third guy stepped up. 'Strange? It's not strange at all. There's no stop because there's no Imabari City any more. It got burned up last April in the air raid. No city, no stop, not strange at all, very natural, very logical. The railroad people are very logical.'

"'No Imabari City . . . burned up,' I said in a depressed voice.

"'That's right,' he continued to explain. 'No buildings, no houses, no people, no nothing but Imabari Station. The whole city burned up and the people ran away. Nothing left in Imabari . . .'

"'All burned down . . .'

"'If the train stops at Imabari Station, what could you do? Nothing, it's very natural for the train to pass.'

"'Oh,' I said. 'Imabari burned down,' and I was so surprised."

His fellow soldier explained to Manabe: "'The air raids came on the 26th of April and the 8th of May. Imabari was burned up. My father was in business there. We had a wholesale drapery business. All gone. All burned up.'

"'Your father?'

"'Dead. Killed in the fire.' He gave a deep sigh.

"'Where will you go when it is over?'

"'Not to Imabari. There's nothing for me there anymore. Everybody is dead.'

"The soldier's life was no life at all," Manabe continued. "The soldier was not provided with newspapers or radio. The soldier did not know what was happening in the rest of the world.

"At the end of this war, only three prefectures in all Japan were left untouched by the bombing: Yamagata, Ishikawa, and Shimane were not attacked.

All the other prefectures, including those in Hokkaido, were attacked, either by carrier bombers or B-29s."

Manabe didn't know that on May 8 Germany had surrendered and that the Second World War had ended in Europe. He was shocked to know that Imabari had disappeared from the earth and he was wondering what had become of Tokyo, Osaka, Nagoya, and other places he knew. Because small cities like Imabari were now targets, all the big cities must be burned up, he thought.

"What has become of the magazine company and my boss, what has become of the novelist Shutaro Kagawa, who was good at historical novels. Will he have a chance to write the history of this war? What has become of my friend Sadai Maruyama. What has become of that girl Kazuko Ochi, living in the apartment in Koishikawa?

"I just wondered how they are. I hope they are fine."

The U.S. Navy warships were now cruising close to the Japanese coast. The carriers had orders to intercept the Kamikazes that were swarming from the Kyushu air bases to attack the ships off Okinawa.

Day after day carrier planes attacked the shores of all the Japanese islands. When they hit the Kochi area, Manabe and his fellow soldiers hid behind rocks or ducked into the caves they were digging.

One day several carrier planes bombed and strafed the area where Manabe was working. He ducked into his cave. One hour later he heard a voice calling: "Soldier Manabe are you there? If you are there give me a reply."

The voice belonged to Soldier Ochi. He had been in Manchuria with the Kwantung Army, but many army units had been transferred, some of them to Okinawa, some to Taiwan, and some to Shikoku. Ochi's unit had come to Shikoku. As an old soldier in the Kwantung Army, Manabe had much in common with Ochi. From time to time they got together to talk.

But Manabe had not seen Ochi for some time. And now here he was, at his digging site. Manabe had resumed digging after the attack and he was deep in the back of the cave. When he heard the shout, Manabe answered and came out.

Both of them ran up to each other and shook hands, a custom they had picked up from foreigners. When Manabe looked at Ochi's shirt badge he found it was changed. Ochi was now a corporal. "Oh!" Manabe said. "You got promoted."

"Yes," Ochi answered. "I have been a soldier for such a long time in Manchuria I deserved it." He was grinning. "We will see each other again some day and have a chat."

But Manabe's unit had no holidays. "*Getsu-getsu ka-sui-moku-kin-kin. Nichi youbiha nai.* Monday, Monday, Tuesday, Wednesday, Thursday, Friday, Friday, Monday again. No Saturday and no Sunday. That's our schedule. So is yours, isn't it? Where are you working?"

Ochi gestured vaguely. "I will visit you. It's all right because I am an officer. I have much more free time than *you* soldiers," Ochi laughed.

The next day he kept his promise and visited Manabe again. Then a miracle happened. Ochi was there, and there was Kazuko Ochi. Manabe remembered that they were brother and sister.

"Oh there you are, Kazuko. What have you been doing?"

She was standing behind Corporal Ochi.

"She came to see me," Ochi said " When I told her Manabe is here, she said she wanted to see Manabe. So I brought her along. Surprised?"

"More than surprised," Manabe said. "It's a miracle. She is supposed to be in Tokyo."

"Her apartment in Tokyo was burned out. She was evacuated," Ochi said. "She came here."

"Oh your apartment was burned in the air raid in Tokyo," Manabe said. He had not greeted her yet, because her arrival was so sudden he was confused. Manabe took a step forward toward Kazuko. "When was the air raid?" he asked.

"The 25th of May," she replied in a low voice, looking down at her feet.

"The 25th of May? I had a red card two months before. I don't really know what has been happening in Tokyo since March. Did the air raids in Tokyo continue after March 9?"

"Yes they did. On the 9th of March Kotoku and the eastern part burned down. On the 25th of May the western part of Tokyo burned down. Now there are no places left to burn down," she said.

Manabe said, "All were burned down weren't they? A few lonely landmarks left in a vast area . . ."

Ochi burst in. "Let's find someplace cool and continue this complicated conversation. I cannot stand this heat."

Manabe said, "Oh you are right. It is noon. I will take a lunch break. I know a very good place where we can take a nap to sabotage work." Manabe pointed out the shade of the rocks on the bank of the river.

It was then he noticed that Kazuko wore *monpei,* made from an old *yukata,* and patched shoes.

17

Kawasaki, Yokohama, and Smaller Cities

As with the other major Japanese cities, the first attack on Kawasaki was the Doolittle raid of April 1942, which was like a blunderbuss, hitting out indiscriminately, injuring and killing civilians, and damaging hospitals and schools rather than military installations.

Two and a half years later, on November 24, 1944, B-29s from the Marianas attacked the Kawanishi aircraft factory and several subsidiary factories in Kawasaki.

The city was a crucial target. Kawasaki was the home of many military supply factories partly because of its central location between Tokyo and Yokohama.

On February 4, 1945, the Americans ran a test attack on Kawasaki, using firebombs. It was successful enough that on March 17 Kawasaki had its first big air raid. Then on May 11 the bombers brought fire to the Kawanishi factory. The company's specialty was big four-engine flying boats.

By the time of the Japanese surrender, the Kawanishi factory had been reduced to what the Japanese called *bakudan no gomi tame*—the rubbish of bombing.

In the middle of the morning on May 29, 1945, Yokohama was hit by 517 B-29s, accompanied by 101 Iwo Jima-based P-51 fighter planes. The B-29s plastered the city with firebombs. Many people were working in Yokohama then, including student workers. Student workers were not always reliable and so the fatality figures are not precise.

The B-29s and P-51s were met by heavy antiaircraft fire and 150 Japanese army and navy fighters, action that had been absent in earlier raids. The counterattack was violent. The Japanese called it the "thunderbolt" maneuver—hit and run.

Navy pilot Lieutenant (j.g.) Ayao Teramura recalled in his memoirs that in the midst of the fight, the pilots of eight Zero fighter "thunderbolts" showed great heroism. Japanese fighters shot down six B-29s, and antiaircraft guns shot down one plane and claimed to have damaged 175 planes. But the P-51s did great damage to the Japanese planes. According to U.S. records, twenty-six Japanese fighters were shot down and nine damaged; twenty-three others suffered unconfirmed damage. It was the biggest air battle since the April 15 raid on Kawasaki.

The planes in the May 29 attack came in from Suruga Bay, and it was said they were so numerous that they blackened the sky. It looked like a great cloud was descending on the city. The center of the city was wiped out during the raid, which lasted an hour and thirty-five minutes. Forty-four percent of Yokohoma City was destroyed that day.

After the six big cities had all been torched, the B-29s turned their attention on smaller targets. Beginning on June 27, 1945, they hit fifty-seven mid-size and small cities in sixteen raids. Sometimes, as in the case of the bombing of Tsu, they telegraphed their punch in an almost obscene manner. If the Japanese air force had been powerful enough, the Americans would have suffered heavy losses. As it was, they went unchallenged.

General LeMay set up the Tsu raid so he could test the effectiveness of the M-47 incendiary, a new bomb. It was the only bomb used during the attack on July 29 on Tsu and Aomori.

Leaflets and radio broadcasts gave advance warning of the attack date. About eighty B-29s were used to attack Tsu.

Tsu residents had been preparing for this attack since June, when it became apparent that Japan's smaller cities were targets. Thousands of families had moved up into the hills above the city. Children and the elderly remained in the hills, while the able-bodied returned to town to fight the fires when the attack came.

On June 18, the bombers attacked Yokkaichi, which was not far from Tsu. Tsu's police chief went there after the attack to learn what he could about the bombs being dropped by U.S. planes.

That city had been attacked with M-69 and M-47 firebombs. The M-69 could be extinguished with water, but the M-47 could not. The police chief returned to Tsu and told the people about the bombs. If M-69 bombs hit the houses, it would make sense to fight the fires. But if the houses were hit by M-47 bombs, fighting the fires would be useless.

Tsu's residents were ready for anything. Since the beginning of the fire-bombing, the Home Ministry and the Ministry of Munitions had collaborated to build an underground aircraft factory at Tsu. The Americans knew nothing about it but the people of Tsu believed they did know, and that was why Tsu had been selected for bombing again. Tsu also had a naval aircraft factory and an arsenal, another factory that had recently been converted to airplane parts manufacture, and three other defense industries. The firebombers had already destroyed their hospital and police station. Most people thought the attack on the hospital was deliberate, but it was actually the result of very poor marksmanship.

On the night of July 27, 1945, the B-29s left Tinian for Tsu. They attacked with firebombs and gutted the city, destroying most of the factories, and they killed 1,498 people. The city was left in flames.

Aomori had first been attacked along with Hokkaido on July 14, 1945, by Admiral William F. Halsey's carrier fleet. The attack by forty Grummans began at 2 o'clock in the morning. The targets were schools, the railroad station, locomotive switchyards, and rolling stock. Patrol boats and several armed steamers on Aomori Bay were attacked; the boat pilots began zigzagging to escape certain death. They had several narrow escapes. Several were sunk or left in sinking condition.

Leaflets announcing the raids were dropped on Tsu and Aomori. By blind luck, most of the leaflets dropped on Tsu floated up into the mountains where the people were. During the Tsu raid, one B-29 flew over Aomori and scattered leaflets that stated: "You are going to have an air raid."

The following day, July 28, sixty-one B-29s attacked Aomori as promised, flying in from Iwo Jima. The radio announced their arrival: "Aomori people, everyone. *Ganbatte kudasai!* Stand firm!"

The voice on the radio continued to shout. After a while the B-29s dropped star shells, and in a wink it was as bright as noon. Fire began to break out here and there. Soon the residential area was alive with flames. As the firebombs rained down, people ran everywhere, their clothes catching fire as they tried to escape the inferno.

The bombing lasted just over an hour, but in that time thousands of firebombs were dropped and 88 percent of Aomori was destroyed; 1,767 people were killed, 282 wounded and 18,000 houses were burned. After that there was nothing left to bomb in Aomori.

The carrier planes came to Kagoshima first on March 18, and by August 6 that city had been bombed eight times. On that first air raid the target was the Koorimoto City Naval Air Base and ships in Kagoshima Bay. The first

B-29 fire raid was on June 17. The planes scattered 12,500 firebombs and created a sea of fire that burned the city's center. More than 2,300 people were killed, 3,500 injured and 11,600 houses burned; 66,000 people were affected.

Bombers and carrier planes attacked Kagoshima railroad station on July 27, and burned out the station's center. The city's western area was also burned out. The bombers were flying at altitudes of 2,300 to 3,000 meters, dropping M-69 and M-47 firebombs. People who were running to escape the attack were pursued by low-flying fighter planes with machine guns. Four hundred and twenty people were killed and more than six hundred were injured.

The next attack was by B-24 bombers, which hit the harbor area; that was followed by another B-29 raid. Twenty percent of the buildings were destroyed.

Okayama was demolished in a morning raid June 29. The raid began at 2:30 in the morning, with 143 B-29s dropping firebombs indiscriminately. Carrier planes also hit the city, before and after the raid. Just one week earlier, on June 22, more than a thousand B-29s had struck the Mitsubishi Mizushima aircraft factory in a bombing attack that lasted three hours. Dozens of nearly completed aircraft were burned up and the factory was demolished. Work at the factory was stopped.

Okayama residents had a feeling the city would be attacked, but the great air raid was very sudden and no warning was given. By the time the air-raid warning was finally sounded, the city was in flames.

Why did the warning come so late? Some army executives stationed in the Okayama area thought the B-29 squadron was heading for Osaka or Kobe, not Okayama. The result of that poor judgment was 1,737 dead, 120,000 wounded and 25,000 damaged houses.

The people of Sendai, the central city of northern Honshu, woke up to air-raid sirens at midnight on July 10. But 124 B-29s had already reached Sendai and were dropping firebombs. The attack lasted two hours.

According to U.S. statistics the B-29s dropped eight high-explosive bombs and 12,961 firebombs, weighing a total of 912 tons. The scattered attack killed 28 people, wounded 385, and demolished 23,956 houses. The central part of the city was destroyed.

By daybreak, fires still burned in the center of the city. People were walking up and down the streets, trying to find family members. Civil defense officials told refugees to go to public shelters. "Don't give up," they said.

In July, U.S. planes scattered leaflets that promised attacks on the people of Mito, Toyama, Hachioji, Kooriyama, Fukuyama , Nagano Kurume, Takaoka, Maebashi, Nishinomiya, Manazuru, and Otsu. The leaflets read:

Notice to the Japanese People

Don't you think that you your brothers and friends must be saved? If you want to be saved then please read this leaflet carefully.

Within a few days we are going to attack military facilities in those cities.

The Japanese army will use weapons manufactured in those factories to continue the losing battle so we are going to destroy all the factories.

But bombs don't have eyes, so we don't know where the bombs will drop. As you know well humanistic Americans don't want to hurt innocent Japanese people, so people who live in these cities please evacuate.

You are not our enemy, our enemy is the Army. Why don't you select a new leader who will end the war?

People in different places named in the leaflet might be bombed, because we will definitely attack at least ten of the twelve cities.

On August 1 at midnight, B-29s flew over Mito, Toyama, and Hachioji. At Hachioji, 169 B-29s struck, killing 2,900 people; at Nagaoka, 125 B-29s attacked, killing 1,490. On August 2 at midnight, 160 B-29s attacked Mito, killing 1,535 people. They hit Toyama with 174 B-29s, killing 5,936.

And the burning of Japan went on.

18

Hiroshima Horror

After Germany surrendered in early May 1945, the Allies turned their attention to Asia and made plans to invade Japan. Six million Americans were to remain on active duty. The U.S. government predicted that the dual invasion of Honshu and Kyushu islands would cost as many as 500,000 lives.

In June General Arnold asked General LeMay when the war was going to end. LeMay's answer: September or October. By then, LeMay said, he would have run out of targets in his drive to burn up Japan. LeMay paid no heed to the Japanese generals' vow to fight on until they received the sort of peace they could claim as victory.

Allied leaders met in June at Potsdam, Germany, and considered the same question. Britain was eager to increase its participation and Stalin wanted the USSR involved so he could share in the loot and perhaps secure a political triumph to match the one he had achieved in Europe. The Americans had perfected the atomic bomb and were considering how to use it. They were woefully uninformed about political developments in Japan, where the emperor had long since decided the war was lost and should be ended.

On July 27, the Allies sent a message—the Potsdam Declaration—to the Japanese government, demanding an immediate unconditional surrender. The declaration made no mention of the status of the emperor, but indicated that he might be charged with war crimes. The principal Japanese military leaders greeted the declaration with disdain. The average Japanese civilian still expected to die fighting.

When the Japanese government did not respond to the Potsdam Declaration, U.S. President Harry Truman decided to drop atomic bombs on Japan to force surrender and "to shorten the agony of war, to save the lives of thousands and thousands of young Americans."

119

Hiroshima was selected as the primary target for the first atomic bomb, with Kokura and Nagasaki as alternate targets in case of bad weather over Hiroshima.

August 6, 1945, dawned bright and sunny over Hiroshima. Takeharu Terao was a third-year student in the mathematics department at Hiroshima Teacher's College. Most of the students at the college had been drafted into the army, until only the top students in science and mathematics remained. But even they had been mobilized to work in the Mitsubishi shipyard in Hiroshima's Eba district. The yard built 10,000-ton troop transports.

Terao had begun as a welder but had been promoted to an instructor. He lived with the other college workers at a Miyajima inn; all of them commuted to the shipyard every day by boat. It was about an hour's ride through dangerous waters that were often mined and subject to frequent attack by U.S. carrier planes. They had made wooden floats to use as life jackets—just in case.

It was already hot by the time the students reached the shipyard that morning. Just before 8 o'clock the air-raid siren sounded and they took cover. The alarm was false and the alert was soon canceled. Work began as usual. Terao was taking attendance in his classroom on the second floor when suddenly a bluish white light flashed through the room and the world went white.

Thinking that there had been a gas explosion, he rushed to the window and saw a yellowish scarlet plume rising like candle fire, high in the sky, surrounded by swirling black smoke. He did not see the mushroom cloud. That came later. At the same time houses rose up off their foundations and collapsed like dominos. He saw a white wave coming toward him (the shock wave). Someone shouted at him and he ducked under the desk and held his breath, waiting. A few seconds later he felt the floor collapse beneath him. He crept out from under the desk.

"Your right eye is hurt," his friend Soma shouted.

He touched his eye and saw blood on his hand but he didn't feel any pain. Blood flowed into his eye and blinded him, so he leaned on Soma's shoulder and was led to the company infirmary, where there was already a queue of about two hundred people, most of them suffering burns. He joined the line and tried to stanch the flow of blood in his eye, but it kept bleeding. His clothes were covered with blood, making it look as though his wound was very serious, and he was moved to the front of the line.

A doctor examined his eye, disinfected it, and put in four stitches. There was nothing wrong with his eyeball. He had been cut by flying glass from the windows, which had disintegrated in front of him.

He was placed on a board, and a tag was put on his chest stating his name, birthplace, age, and blood type, and then he was placed among the other wounded. People all around him were groaning with pain and crying out for water; some of them were dying. The only burn remedy available was a white salve, which was applied to all burns. As the hours wore on, their suppurating wounds began to stink.

At about 3 o'clock that afternoon the Enamimaru Ferry came to pick them up and he returned to the inn in Miyajima. The next morning the healthy people were ordered to Hiroshima City to help with the clean-up work, but the injured were left in quarters to rest.

Terao rested on August 7, but the next day he went into the shipyard at Eba with friends, and then over to Hiroshima City to see what had happened. His head, except for his left eye, was wrapped in bandages. He went first to his Aunt and Uncle Matsuoka's house in the Minami Kannon district, where he had stayed. Nothing there; the house had been pulverized and there was no sign of the family. He never discovered what had happened to them.

He wandered down to the school at Higashisendamachi. The school had been incinerated; only parts of the concrete walls were left. All around him were dead bodies, and a few people checking the bodies to see if any relatives were there.

The town was filled with the stink of death.

He came to a bridge, where Akatsuki unit soldiers were picking bodies out of the stream, using landing craft. All the bodies were naked, some of them twisted in agony, white and bloated. He turned away from the scene.

He walked to the Takano Bridge and crossed over to get to his college. All the wooden buildings, dormitories, and classrooms were gone, burned up. Only the library and the science building remained. At the side of the front entrance was the body of a horse that had turned putrid in two days.

Terao's next stop was the house of his friends the Hashimotos, whom he had helped to build an underground bomb shelter. The house was burned up. The shelter was intact and someone had come and retrieved belongings, so he felt that the Hashimoto women had survived. The husband, his friend, had gone off to war, and Terao never saw him again. Later he returned to Hiroshima and asked around, but found no trace of the family.

He walked down to Shirigamisha, along the streetcar avenue, to the municipal square. In the square was a burned-out streetcar, with wires swinging inside the window. There he received a Sufferer's Certificate, attesting to his injury in the atomic bombing. He did not feel embarrassed at being swathed in bandages. Nearly everyone on the street was bandaged, and many were "wandering around like zombies."

He turned left at the Kamiya crossing and walked on through the wreckage of the Hiroshima Prefectural Industrial Promotion Hall (later called the A-bomb dome), the T-shaped Bridge of Aioi, Dobashi and the Fukushima District, and toward the Ibi District.

Everywhere, as far as the eye could see, was the evidence that a once-thriving city was now a charnel house. The city was burned to ashes, amid which the relics of buildings stood, bare walls and bits of walls. In one window several blackened tin plates clattered in the wind. He walked past hundreds of meters of debris, avoiding the dead bodies, most of which were now covered with rugs and pieces of cloth.

Finally he arrived at Ibi station. The station was as quiet as a tomb, for that is what it was: a tomb filled with rotting corpses. At the station he boarded a Miyajima streetcar and returned to the inn.

Every day for the next week he walked around what had once been a bustling, living city but was now a deserted wasteland. Later he had regrets over what he termed "my foolish behavior." He hoped never again to witness such sights, he did not even want to remember them, and he shut off his memory for years before he finally wrote a brief memoir.

The debate over surrender continued in Japan, with the militarists unalterably opposed. On the morning of August 9, Soviet Union troops marched into Manchukuo and began the campaign against the remnants of the Kwantung Army.

19

Nagasaki Nightmare

On August 9, the Americans prepared to drop their second atomic bomb, this time on Kokura, on the northern tip of Kyushu. Kokura was selected because it was the site of an important Japanese army arsenal. But the weather over Kokura was very cloudy and, after three separate bombing runs, the bombardier gave up. The U.S. military turned to its secondary target: Nagasaki.

On August 9, 1945, Dr. Raisuke Shirabe, professor of surgery at Nagasaki Medical College, was on duty as supervisor of the air-raid guard. He was standing in for Professor Takase, who was absent. He got up at 6 o'clock that morning, dressed as usual, and joined three other professors at breakfast at 6:30 in the hospital dining room.

An air-raid alarm sounded at 7 o'clock. Dr. Shirabe assembled the students on duty in front of the main building and called roll, then sent them off to their posts to watch for aircraft. When no aircraft had appeared by 9 o'clock, the alarm was reduced to an alert and the day's routine began.

Still wearing his air-raid gaiters, Dr. Shirabe went to the second lecture hall for a class with third-year medical students. After class, he passed the main lecture hall and saw that, while the dean's lecture was over, the dean and students were still talking.

Dr. Shirabe was writing in his office when he heard the distant sound of an airplane's engines. He changed quickly from his laboratory coat into his suit jacket and gathered up his belongings to go to the air-raid shelter. Just as he reached his office door, a silvery-purple light flashed in the windows on the north side of the building.

He heard a crash; the room fell in on him and he passed out. When he regained consciousness he was on the floor. The ceiling had fallen on him and he was covered with plaster. He heard a sound like rain and realized that it was dirt falling on the roof, dirt that had been sucked up by a tremendous explosion.

He struggled to his feet and opened his eyes. He couldn't see anything. He felt abandoned. He crouched on the floor and waited. Then he got up again. There was a little light, and he could see that his desk had fallen on its side and the ceiling had fallen onto the floor. The bookshelves had toppled over, and the bed was askew. He went to the desk and picked up his diary, which had been shredded, and put it in his pocket. He could not find his briefcase, and all the objects that had been on the desk had disappeared. He made his way downstairs and out the building, and then saw a woman on whom he had operated recently. She was calling for help but she didn't seem to have any external injuries. He told her to get away from the building and went on. "You're all right, don't worry," he called to her.

The college's boiler shed had been crushed, and escaping steam was whistling. Several people were lying on the concrete platform in front of the shed. Dr. Shirabe also saw bodies hanging out of the hospital windows.

He met Professor Koyano on the way to the air-raid shelter. Koyano had superficial cuts, caused by flying glass, but did not seem to be hurt too badly. They exchanged remarks and he went on.

The shelter was filled with people, so Dr. Shirabe went back to the main building where a crowd was just emerging. It was impossible to squeeze through the throng. He decided to climb the hill in back of the hospital. At this time, he noticed that he didn't have even a scratch on his body.

Next he met a graduate student named Satoh, who was walking with a nurse and supporting himself with a stick. He had no apparent injuries, but the nurse's face was stained with blood and her *monpei* were ripped open at the hip. He told them to continue up to the top of the hill.

He decided to return to his office, and while crossing the tennis court met Professor Hasegawa, who had a wound on his right shoulder and was bleeding. "Keep pressure on the wound until it stops bleeding," he told Hasegawa and continued on his way,

Dr. Shirabe started running, but Dr. Ishizaki, an assistant professor, came crawling toward him, calling his name. Dr. Ishizaki had terrible wounds all over his face, and skin was hanging down from his forearms and hands.

"Where were you when it happened?" Dr. Shirabe asked him.

"In my office."

"There's nothing to worry about. Stay here and rest with Dr. Hasegawa."

Dr. Shirabe then started for the east wing of the hospital. He met Dr. Kido, whose wounds were slight, and Mrs. Murayama, the head nurse, who was screaming his name. She had burns on her arms and face. "It's so good to see you alive," Dr. Shirabe said to her. "Let's go up to the top of the hill together."

The nurses in the surgery department had escaped injury, Dr. Shirabe was told, so he decided not to return to the hospital. He started up the hill, supporting Mrs. Murayama on his shoulder.

Fires had broken out in the ruins of the hospital and wooden buildings in the area. The hill was covered with smoke and it was like trying to walk through a thick fog. The ground, which had been covered the day before with thick vegetation, was now stripped bare.

A boys' reformatory on the other side of the hill had been demolished and the ruins were on fire. People were crying for help and moaning. It was like a portrait of the agonies of hell in a Buddhist iconography. The wind was blowing down the mountain, carrying clouds of black smoke up and pushing the procession of hideously injured people toward the illusion of safety.

As they reached the hillside where the boys' reformatory had been, Dr. Shirabe heard someone calling his name. It was Dr. Tsunoh, the dean, who was lying injured somewhere on the mountain. Shirabe told his companions to go ahead without him, and then cut across the rocks, toward the voice.

He found Dr. Tsunoh on the ground, surrounded by Drs. Osashima and Takahashi, and a nurse named Maeda. Tsunoh's face was ashen and his shirt was stained with blood. "Where are you hurt?" Dr. Shirabe asked him.

"My left arm and leg. It's nothing," the dean said.

Dr. Shirabe offered words of encouragement and bandaged the dean's wounds. He stripped off the bloody shirt and gave the dean his own shirt. The doctors and nurse couldn't stay where they were, he said. They must seek shelter.

Dr. Takahashi looked to be the strongest of the group, so he carried Dr. Tsunoh. As they climbed the hill, they had to pause several times because Dr. Tsunoh felt faint and nauseated.

The boys' reformatory buildings were a mass of flames. They heard many cries for help from victims, some of them naked, some of them covered by the remnants of clothing, some hideously burned, some streaming with blood.

They finally reached an old potato field halfway up Mount Konpira and put Dr. Tsunoh down on a patch of wilted sweet potato. Someone found a quilt and they covered him. The wind was strong and he seemed to be chilled.

Before long Dr. Okura, who hadn't been injured, arrived and built a flag stand out of potato stems to mark the "emergency" hospital.

The wind shifted and began to blow toward the city. The smoke dissipated, allowing for a clear view of the hospital complex. The nurses' dormitory, outdoor corridors, and medical school buildings were engulfed in raging fires. The sun was a sick reddish brown in color.

Someone brought a first-aid kit that contained tincture of iodine. Dr. Shirabe used the iodine to treat Dr. Tsunoh's wounds. The wind shifted again and brought rain. The injured people on the hill were now wet *and* cold.

Dr. Shirabe took a few minutes to search for his second son, Koji, a first-year medical student. Shirabe called his son's name. When there was no response, he decided the boy had been trapped in the lecture hall and had died.

The roads and fields were scattered with hideously injured people. Most of them didn't have the energy to speak. Among them he noticed a fourth-year student named Oku who was obviously dying and made no effort to answer his call. Rainwater dripped from his face.

A voice called to Dr. Shirabe: "Please, come back." He returned to Dr. Tsunoh and found Dr. Nagai on the ground with a cut near his right ear. "We can't stop the bleeding," one of the people said. Several hemostats were hanging from the wound. Dr. Shirabe tried to stop the bleeding, but couldn't.

Someone brought a piece of ice, which they gave the dean in a cup made of half a squash. The dean ate it with relish, obviously thirsty.

At about 4 o'clock a student named Koda arrived carrying Professor Takahashi on his back. Takahashi had no visible wounds but seemed exhausted and in great pain. He had been trapped in his office, then had fled across the fields to Urakami Cathedral, where he had collapsed and where Koda had found him.

Finally, the rain stopped and the wind died down. The hillside was enveloped in a soft evening mist. But the fires in the city burned brighter than ever. The medical school refugees settled down for the night in two groups, one around Dr. Tsunoh, and the other around Dr. Nagai.

Emergency relief teams arrived with a case of dry bread that Dr. Shirabe distributed. Down the hill, he saw that a medical student named Ando had organized a kitchen and was cooking rice in a big pot. Several young women in wartime work clothes, students organized to work in the Mitsubishi factories, were helping him.

When the rice was cooked, Drs. Shirabe and Ando went back up the hill, distributing rice balls as they went, to where Dr. Tsunoh was resting. They ate and settled down for the night.

Dr. Shirabe wondered what had become of his two sons. Koji had been in the middle of a lecture. Had he survived? His eldest son Seiichi had gone to work as usual at the Ohashi arms factory. Was he all right?

The next morning dawned hot and clear. They brought Drs. Tsunoh and Takaki to the hospital on stretchers, but the buildings were mostly burned down. The whole complex was in such confusion that they carried the doctors into a cave air-raid shelter that had been turned into an emergency clinic.

On his way to what had been his office, Dr. Shirabe saw bodies everywhere—in the corridors of the ruined building, even in the potato fields.

When he returned to his home, he found his wife, his son Seiichi, and three daughters. Seiichi was bandaged from head to toe. Koji had not returned. His eighty-year-old mother had not been hurt. The house was located four kilometers from the hypocenter of the explosion, but still all the ceilings had fallen in and all the windows and paper screens had been destroyed.

Dr. Shirabe decided to establish a relief station downtown and found space at the Iwaya Club. He found medicine and undamaged instruments in the hospital's wreckage and had them brought to the clinic site.

The Iwaya Clinic opened on August 13, and Dr. Tsunoh was one of the first patients. His wounds began to show signs of infection, and he was experiencing high fevers, bloody stools, and symptoms of dysentery. Dr. Shirabe's son, Seiichi, came down with the same symptoms.

On August 15, Dr. Shirabe heard the dejecting news that the war was over. Several of his patients died.

Seiichi died on August 16. Dr. Tsunoh's diarrhea became worse, and he was running a fever of 41 degrees C. (105.8 degrees F.).

People were saying that U.S. forces would soon begin landing. Dr. Shirabe's neighbors began to flee from the city to Mount Iwaya, and he was urged to do the same. "Even the police are leaving the city," his informant said. The nurses begged that they be allowed to go home, to try to escape the occupation forces. Dr. Shirabe decided it was time to close the clinic.

Dr. Tsunoh was taken to the nearby Shinto shrine, and the other patients and clinic workers were sent away. Dr. Tsunoh was suffering from an unknown disease that is now called radiation sickness. He died on August 22.

Dr. Shirabe found his son Koji's remains at the lecture area on August 28. Koji was identified by his trousers, which were hand-me-downs from his cousin Yamamoto, whose name was written on the waistband. This was all that was left of Koji.

Many people became ill from the radiation sickness, including Dr. Shirabe, who grew weaker as the days went on. On September 16, one of his associates ran a test on his white and red blood cells. His white blood count was very high. He was later diagnosed with radiation sickness, but his was a mild case and he soon recovered.

Dr. Shirabe enjoyed a distinguished career with many honors, including being named dean of the medical school. He continued to work with radiation cases and was active in the Radiation Effects Research Foundation. He was awarded the Order of the Sacred Treasure, second class, by the emperor in 1971. He died in 1989 at the age of eighty-nine.

20

To Shorten the War

General LeMay said his aim in burning up Japan was to shorten the war by forcing Japan's quick surrender, but the effect of the firebombing was quite the opposite. By April 1945, most Japanese believed they were going to die anyhow and responded when the government called on them to prepare to fight on the beaches.

The unconditional surrender sought by the Allies was anathema to the Japanese generals and civilians alike. To surrender unconditionally meant losing their emperor and the imperial system.

In cities and towns the Japanese people prepared for the "decisive battle," training with staves as hundreds of home factories manufactured simple grenades that a woman or child could throw under a tank or a truck. Some women were training as sharpshooters.

The number of firebombings decreased in April and May, when the U.S. Joint Chiefs of Staff gave new orders to LeMay. Instead of conducting air raids, the B-29s were to sow mines in Japanese waters, and then support the invasion of Okinawa with raids on Kyushu, Honshu, and Taiwan airfields— the lairs of the Kamikazes. General LeMay cooperated at first, but after a few raids on Kyushu he decided that the job was finished and that it was time to get back to burning up Japan. General Arnold stopped him, with the support of General Marshall and Admiral King.

One thing LeMay wanted to do was finish the job in Tokyo. After the March 9 firestorm, the Home Ministry realized that the firebombs posed a new kind of danger and so instituted a drastic change in Tokyo's civil defense system. They took a clue from Nagoya where the city fathers had laid out firebreaks.

Whole city blocks in Tokyo were to be destroyed to create fire lanes. Officials moved through the wards, marking houses with the word "execute" or fastening chains on the doors. The residents were given a week to evacuate. On the appointed day a wrecking crew, usually women and students, showed up. The crew fastened a heavy cable to the house and began to pull on it. Usually that was enough to bring down one of the flimsy Tokyo houses, but if not a truck or an army tank would be brought in to do the job.

When the work was complete twenty firebreaks had been created in Tokyo, each one hundred to two hundred meters wide; eighty more, each fifty meters wide, went through the center of the capital.

The U.S. bombers had not paid much attention to transportation facilities yet. Tokyo's railroad station was cleared, as was the area for blocks around. The city could not afford to have a burned-out railroad station. It was the center of the Japanese rail industry. All trains went through Tokyo, no matter which direction.

Toyohama is a village near the small city of Hamamatsu in Shizuoka, with greenhouses, fisherman, factories, and farms. In times of trouble the people living there were supposed to evacuate to the pine forest on the bay.

Hiroko Kato was a sixth-grade student in that summer of 1945, when the air raids were becoming fiercer each day. One day in June, at about 4 o'clock in the afternoon, the bombers arrived at Hamamatsu. Toyohama village officials knew how widely the bombs would be scattered and told residents to evacuate the village.

Hiroko had never experienced anything so frightening, not even an earthquake. Everything was chaos. The air-raid siren blared. Civil defense people were shouting. "Our enemy has begun shooting. Please hurry to evacuate to the pine trees. Everybody get ready."

Her father loaded futons, blankets, food, water, and other supplies into the family's wooden wagon. Hiroko's younger brother and sister were jammed on top. Her father began to pull the heavy wagon along the dirt road. The line of evacuees was long and people became very impatient. "Hurry up, hurry up, hurry up!" they shouted from behind.

Finally the Kato family reached the pine trees, exhausted and sweating. The bay was full of U.S. warships. The B-29s were attacking from the air and the U.S. Third Fleet was bombarding the shore. "Our enemy is just in front of us. We are going to lose," people in the crowd cried.

It grew dark. When Hiroko climbed up to the bank she saw three ships in the bay, their guns shooting at the shore. Years later, she still remembered the scene clearly: the red flashes from the gun barrels and the crackling sound of the shells exploding in Hamamatsu.

Hamamatsu is the second-largest city in Shizuoka prefecture. During the war it housed aircraft and weapons factories, which were targeted by the U.S. ships. First the planes dropped flares, then shots were fired from the ships. The sky above Hamamatsu turned red. Hiroko Kato watched from the distance until the firing stopped.

That night, mosquitoes attacked, keeping Hiroko awake. The next morning she stood on the bank and looked out at the bay where a big, black carrier floated. She sat in the forest for a long time, watching that carrier and thinking.

Hiroko returned to the forest often in the weeks to come, to contemplate the damage being done to her country, and wonder what the future would hold.

LeMay's B-29s had bombed the capital several times since the great raid of March 9. Most notable was the attack on May 24, when the bombers hit the Imperial Palace and most of the government district of western Tokyo.

U.S. President Harry Truman wasn't through with Tokyo, however. When Japan didn't surrender after the atomic bombs were dropped on Hiroshima and Nagasaki, plans were made to drop a third atomic bomb—this one on Tokyo. Not content with that, General LeMay continued his attacks until the end, destroying Japanese cities of all sizes.

Meanwhile, in Japan the subject of surrender was being furiously debated. The emperor had decided in March that surrender was the only option, but he was constitutionally proscribed from acting. His role was to sanction decisions made by the Cabinet.

On August 13, the six-man Japanese Supreme War Council met and debated the issue. Three members favored surrender and three, led by War Minister Anami, were opposed. The meeting produced nothing. Their decision would have been meaningless anyhow. The only governmental body that could decide to surrender was the Cabinet, and its decision had to be unanimous.

The sixteen-man Cabinet also met on August 13, and twelve voted for surrender; three opposed surrender and one was undecided. At issue: the fate of the emperor and the imperial system. The Japanese had already requested that they be allowed to keep the emperor.

"Our terms are 'unconditional,'" President Truman wrote in his diary on August 10. However, although it was not stated, it was understood that the U.S. government would allow the emperor to stay.

The Cabinet met again on August 14. This time, Emperor Hirohito, who was not a brave man, screwed up his courage and opted to throw himself at the mercy of his conquerors. "It is my desire," he said, "that you, my ministers of state, accede to my wishes and forthwith accept the Allied reply."

The Cabinet's decision was unanimous. On the War Council, General Anami, the leading opponent of surrender, said, "As a Japanese soldier I must obey my emperor."

The next day Hirohito addressed a shocked nation, which had never heard his voice before, and told them that they must lay down their arms. "We must bear the unbearable," he told them.

On August 15, the B-29s flew over Osaka's Kyobashi station, as they had for three days, and dropped more bombs. The trains were full of evacuees, people going anywhere to get out of Osaka. Since there were no men left, schoolgirl volunteers were supervising the evacuation.

One of the stationmasters was Taneko Yamazaki, a high school girl. The Americans were now dropping one-ton, high-explosive bombs. In the attack on August 15, Taneko managed to get into the air-raid shelter before four bombs destroyed the station. The shelter was made of wooden railroad ties and was very strong. When Taneko and the other girl stationmasters came out of the shelter, they discovered they were the only ones who survived the raid.

Kyobashi station was a two-storied building with big stone pillars. These pillars disintegrated in the bombing and became shrapnel, which hit people waiting to board the trains. Taneko came out of the shelter and was frozen in place by what she saw. Corpses and people who were still alive were under rocks.

She couldn't rescue the victims who were still alive. She should have asked their names and addresses, but she was so shocked that she didn't think of it. That was her regret for forty years after the war, she said.

The schoolgirls helped carry the dead on stretchers to a nearby factory. When they reached the factory they heard about the emperor's broadcast and Japan's surrender. The war was over. But some of the Japanese people still wanted to fight.

Taneko returned to the factory the next day. Three days of bombing had left holes, ten meters in diameter, in the factory yard, making it look like a beehive. Dead horses had been thrown into the holes along with piles and piles of documents that were being burned, under the supervision of soldiers. "You may burn anything. You must burn everything," the commanding officer told them.

It took five hours to burn all the documents. At the end of the day, the workers—all of whom were women, mostly schoolgirls, Taneko noticed— were called to assemble.

"I think our enemies will be landing soon," Captain I, the stationmaster staff officer, told them. "From now on you girls must disguise yourselves as men for your own protection. If you are recognized as a woman, you must commit suicide." Then he told them how to go about killing themselves.

"First, you take the blade between your index and middle finger, like this," he said as he illustrated with a flat blade. "You close your eyes and hold your ear lobe and count one, two, three, and slit from top to bottom, cutting off your ear and opening the carotid artery. It will all be over in a moment.

"This is the last parting on earth," he said. "But we military men are supposed to go into the battle. I'm sure we will never meet again, so this is good-bye . . ." And he gave the girls a military salute and then dismissed them.

When Taneko got home, she went to her room and practiced committing suicide. She cut up a heavy file folder to make a blade. She followed the captain's instructions and after a few tries she was able to come down behind her ear, and hit where the carotid artery was supposed to be.

Now she just needed to get a real blade.

Taneko's mother and father talked her out of committing suicide, and she soon learned that American GIs were not the demons painted by Imperial officials. She returned to school in her school uniform and was never accosted.

For a while she wondered what had become of Captain I. Had he, like General Anami, General Sugiyama, Admiral Ohnishi, and Admiral Ugaki, committed suicide, or like General Tojo, tried and bungled the job? Had he gone into futile battle and been killed?

She looked out a school window one morning and had her answer. There in the schoolyard stood a jeep surrounded by her schoolmates. Sitting in the passenger seat was Captain I, dressed in a Hawaiian shirt and chewing gum. Next to him was an American driver.

"Look, girls," the captain said. "I can speak English."

21

Shock

When the U.S. occupation forces arrived to take control of a defeated Japan, they were appalled at what they saw—a nation in complete disarray.

Marine Sergeant Joe O'Donnell was a combat photographer who had orders to document the effects of the bombing on Japan's cities. He waded ashore from a transport in Sasebo Harbor, camera in hand, and began right there.

Sasebo, one of the smaller cities of Japan, was no longer functioning. It had been bombed on June 28, in the third fire raid against smaller cities and towns, along with Okayama, Moji, and Nobeoka. Most of the major buildings had been destroyed. The tall buildings, into which the people rushed for safety, had become ovens, roasting the women and children inside. Nearly three months later the stink of the rotting bodies was still overwhelming. Skeletons of trees that would never bloom again lined the main thoroughfare in arboreal precision.

O'Donnell traveled around Japan for seven months. His pictures of desolation and human misery so depressed him that, after he returned to the United States and was discharged from the Marine Corps, he threw all the negatives into a trunk and vowed never to look at them again. He later became a White House photographer. But during all those years he had nightmares about what he had seen: an old man dying of radiation burns after the Nagasaki atom bomb, hungry and homeless children, ragged families with nothing but the clothes on their backs, the utter wretchedness of a society destroyed.

After retiring, he unlocked the trunk, and prepared a photo exhibit that was shown first in Nashville, and later in other parts of the United States, Europe, and Japan. The exhibit was published as a book in Japan, with a narrative written by Jennifer Alldredge, and titled *Japan—Images from a Trunk* (Tokyo: Shogakukan, 1995).

The book is a record of General LeMay's successful efforts to burn up Japan, topped by what LeMay called the "icing on the cake": the two atomic bombs on Hiroshima and Nagasaki. A look at this book should be enough to make every American cringe in shame.

22

Japan Burned Up

In 1973, Dr. Shigeru Kubota published his study titled *The Great Tokyo Air Raid of March 9, 1945* (Tokyo: Ushio Shuppansha, 1973). In it he claimed that this single firebombing killed and wounded more people than the two atomic bombs combined. There seems no reason to doubt his claim, considering the fragmentary state of Japanese records.

Certainly the firebombing of Japanese cities destroyed millions of homes and accomplished what General LeMay had set out to do: burn up Japan. In a greater sense the firebombing and the atomic bombing were garments cut from the same bolt of cloth. What the bombings left behind was astounding: 330,000 civilians killed; 476,000 civilians wounded; 6 million civilians displaced; and, according to the U.S. Strategic Bombing Survey, at least 2.51 million houses destroyed.

The same claim was made for the firebombings and atomic bombings: that they were humanitarian gestures, made to shorten the war and reduce the number of casualties on both sides.

Around the world, people reacted to the atomic bombings with horror. The reaction to the firebombing was less pronounced. The U.S. reaction to both was the same: justification. The U.S. military continued to produce firebombs and atomic bombs, and even contemplated using atomic bombs in the Korean War. The only thing that stopped those plans was the knowledge that the Soviet Union had atomic weapons and would retaliate, bringing death and destruction to U.S. cities.

It now seems evident that firebombing Japan was unnecessary and had little impact on the outcome of the war. According to the U.S. Strategic Bombing

Survey, "By August 1945 without air attack Japanese war production would have declined below the (wartime high) level of 1944 by 50 percent."

It was the U.S. submarine campaign, not the firebombing, that wrecked the Japanese economy. And neither campaign destroyed Japan's military capability. At the Pacific war's end, the Japanese had more than twice as a many operational aircraft as they had at the start of the war. They began with 2,575 aircraft and ended with 5,000, plus 5,400 Kamikaze planes. At the end of the war, 97 percent of Japan's military supplies were protected either underground or in facilities not vulnerable to air attack. So much for General LeMay's contention that he was attacking military targets.

As for General LeMay's explanation that Japan relied on cottage industry for its war production, making the civil population part of the war machine, the U.S. Strategic Bombing Survey had this to say: "By 1944 Japan had almost totally eliminated home industry in the war economy."

What the strategic bombers should have done was concentrate on the railroads, which they had just begun to do in mid-August, when the war ended. Another part of the Japanese economy that went relatively untouched was the power supply. Germany's power supply was the subject of repeated attacks, but only one-seventh of Japan's power supply was touched, and this included twenty-six steam plants. No effort was made to go after dams or the hydroelectric system. Instead, 40 percent of the built-up areas of sixty-six cities was destroyed. Thirty percent of Japanese civilians who lived in cities lost their houses and many of them also lost all their possessions. The 806,000 civilian casualties of the war outnumbered the 780,000 military casualties.

The Americans were quite right to be concerned about the number of casualties if Japan had been invaded. Two million Japanese soldiers with 97 percent of the nation's war material and more than 9,000 aircraft were waiting for them and knew approximately where they would land. It would have been a bloody battle to the death, as had been promised by the Japanese generals.

Afterword

Was dropping two atomic bombs the only way the Allies could win the war without sacrificing a quarter of a million American lives in an invasion of Japan?

Doug Long, who studied the records and has published works on the atomic bombs, wrote a two-part article that appears on the following Web site: http://mercury.he.net/~dlong/hiroshim.htm. In his conclusion, he quotes General Dwight D. Eisenhower: "It is likely that Dwight Eisenhower was right when he said of the atomic bombings of Japan, 'It wasn't necessary to hit them with that awful thing.'"

But what were the alternatives? There were at least three:

1. Give Prince Konoye the text of the Potsdam Declaration, prior to its release, and give him a week to secure his government's acceptance of it.
2. Pursue the relationship that Alan Dulles had developed in Switzerland with the Japanese groups seeking peace, Fujimura and Okamoto.
3. Inform the Japanese that one atomic bomb could destroy an entire city, even offering proof from the American test.

But none of these alternatives was seriously considered. The reason became apparent fifty years later in the furor caused by the Smithsonian Institute's proposed anniversary exhibition called "Enola Gay, the Story of the Atomic Bombing of Japan." The exhibit was scrapped after thousands of complaints were received from citizens who justified the use of the atomic bombs.

As Doug Long wrote in his article, the U.S. approach was strictly military.

The reason for emphasis on military solutions, as opposed to diplomatic efforts, may lie in the emotionalism and the desire for revenge that accompanies war.

Many found the revenge satisfying regardless of the loss of additional American lives spent to achieve it.

President Harry Truman described the U.S. reaction after Nagasaki:

Having found the bomb, we have used it. We have used it against those who attacked us without warning at Pearl Harbor, against those who have starved and beaten and executed American prisoners of war, against those who abandoned all pretense of obeying international laws of warfare.

So revenge was the real answer to the bomb. But the victims of the atomic bombs and the firebombing of Japan were none of the villains described above. The victims were women, children, and the elderly.

General Haywood S. Hansell, LeMay's predecessor as commander of the XXI Bomber Command, wrote a critique in which he questioned the necessity of the firebombing campaign altogether.

It seems to me in retrospect that the urban incendiary attacks which were more devastating by far than the two atomic attacks, could almost certainly have been avoided or their quantity greatly reduced if primary reliance on selective attacks had been pursued, even if the end of the war were slightly postponed.

Who, then, is responsible for the decision to burn up Japan? The finger points at General LeMay and General Arnold as the unindicted war criminals. In any event, Americans should look on the firebombing and their atomic heritage with shame.

This same callous mindset has persisted in 1999 in the undeclared air war against Serbia that has cost so many civilian lives and caused so much misery. The U.S. Air Force boasts that it has developed "smart" bombs that can pinpoint an objective. That being true, it must also be true that the Air Force targeted civilians in this air war—a war crime.

The war against Serbia should be a subject of American shame. The war was not sanctioned by the United Nations, but was an adventure of NATO and the United States. It is a manifestation of a bullying nation that disguises as altruism a foreign policy that is turning the world against the United States.

Notes

Foreword

I used my own *Japan's War* (New York: McGraw Hill, 1986); Wilbur H. Morrison's *Point of No Return* (New York: Time Books, 1979); the records of the U.N. Commission on the International Criminal Court and the treaty that evolved from it; and Ian Williams's article "Criminal Neglect," *The Nation,* August 10, 1998.

Introduction

Sources were my *Japan's War, Aleutians;* my *The Night Tokyo Burned* (New York: St. Martin's Press, 1987); Motoyuki Manabe's *Tokyo's Great Air Raids* (Tokyo: Kokudo Sha, 1976); and General Curtis LeMay and MacKinley Kantor's *Mission with LeMay* (New York: Doubleday, 1965).

Chapter 1

I used *Japan's War* for background, and Manabe's *Tokyo's Great Air Raids,* Morrison's *Point of No Return,* and my *The Night Tokyo Burned* for information on preparing the B-29s.

This chapter depended on Morrison, Manabe, and Shigeru Kubota (*Tokyo Great Air Raid* [Tokyo: Ushio Shuppansha, 1973]).

The story of taking the machine guns off the B-29s is from Morrison.

The stories about Toshiko Higashikawa, Koji Kikushima and Sumiko Morikawa are from *The Night Tokyo Burned.*

Manabe's Toshiko Tsurumaki's stories are from Manabe's book, *Tokyo's Great Air Raids.*

The following were interviewed by me in 1986 for their stories: Kimie Ono, Miwa Koshiba, Hiratsuka Saki, Masatake Obata, Masuko Harina, Chiyoko Sakamoto, Hideyoshi Kaneko, Seizo Hashimoto, and Tekeiro Ueba.

Stories from Kubota's book: Kinsuke Wakabayama, Chiyoko Yokozawa, Shimizu's story about the American gasoline, Hiyoshi Inoue (confirmed by Juhira Shimizu), and Kubota's own.

Chapter 2

This chapter depended on Morrison and LeMay.

Chapter 3

This chapter relied on the Kubota book, the Miwa and Obata interviews, *The Night Tokyo Burned,* and Katsumoto Saotome's *Mothers and Children in the Great Tokyo Air Raid* (Tokyo: Heibunsha, 1983).

Chapter 4

Kubota was the source here.

Chapter 5

The principal sources were my books, *Japan's War* and *Hirohito* (Westport, Conn.: Praeger, 1992). The Imperial reaction to the firebombing of Tokyo was deep shock.

Chapter 6

I used Morrison and LeMay and the records of the XX Air Force at Maxwell Air Force Base, Alabama, in this chapter.

Chapter 7

My interviews in Nagoya were the source for this chapter.

Chapter 8

My interviews with Miwa Koshiba and Masatake Obate, and the Kubota book, were sources.

Chapter 9

The Kubota book was the basic source.

Chapter 10

The files of the *Japan Times* and *The Night Tokyo Burned* were sources here.

Chapter 11

I relied on *The Night Tokyo Burned* and the Osaka air-raid history book, from which the tales of the leaflet raid, the false raid on Osaka railroad station, and the stories of the Imaio family, the Oshimas, and Toshie Kondo were extracted. The story of Osaka's growth and past is from *Japan's War.*

Chapter 12

The Kobe air-raid book was essential here. I relied on my Kobe interviews for personal stories.

Chapter 13

My interviews with the editors of *Chunichi Shimbun* and with Sensako Sugiyama were essential here, as was *The Night Tokyo Burned.*

Chapter 14

My sources were Kubota's book, materials about the bombing of the Imperial Palace (supplied by the Japan Foreign Press Center), and *Japan's War.* Manabe's book tells the story of Kazuko Ochi.

Chapter 15

The information about the B-29 that was shot down and the stories of Taneko Fujikura, Kiyoko Imajos, and Yoshiko Yamano are from the Osaka air-raid book. Takeo Ikuma's story is from the Kobe air-raid book.

Chapter 16

Manabe's adventures in Kochi are from his book.

Chapter 17

The stories of the firebombing of Kawasaki, Yokohama, Tsu, Aomori, Kagoshima, Okayama, Sendai, and the leaflet story are from Masao Hiratsuka's *American Records of the Air Raids on Japan* (Tokyo: Soushisha, 1995).

Chapter 18

The story of the atomic bombing of Hiroshima is from an online article on the Internet.

Chapter 19

The story of the atomic bombing on Japan is well known. I have chosen to use accounts that are not well known, because in their simplicity they reflect the true horror of the bombing. For the material on the Potsdam Conference and the decision to drop the atomic bombs, I used Morrison's book. Dr. Shirabe's story is from his reminiscences of the Nagasaki atomic bomb on the Internet (http://www-sdc.med.nagasaki-u.ac.jp/n50/shirabe/contents-E.html).

Chapter 20

The account of General LeMay's rationale comes from Morrison and LeMay. The material about the fire lanes in Tokyo is from Manabe's book. The story of the firebombing of Hamamatsu and its effect on the villagers of Toyohama is from Keizabur Kobayshi's *Senka ni Ikita Chichi Haha tachi* (Parents who survived during the war) (Tokyo: Taihei Shuppansha, 1972).

The story of the debate within the Japanese government is from my *Closing the Circle* (Avon, N.Y.: 1975). The story of Taneko Yamazaki and Captain I is from Hiratsuka's book.

Chapter 21

Marine combat photographer Joe O'Donnell was assigned to photograph the impact of the bombing on the Japanese. His photos were later organized as an exhibit and became the basis for a picture book, *Japan 1945: Pictures from a Trunk,* published in Japan.

Chapter 22

Kubota's book is the source for the material about the comparative values of the firebombing and atomic bombing.

Chapter 23

The article by Doug Long on the Internet triggered my reaction and the linking of the atomic bombing to the firebombing campaign. General LeMay rose to become chief of staff of the U.S. Air Force and was awarded the First Class Order of the Grand Cordon of the Rising Sun by Emperor Hirohito, an irony that escaped Americans but was resented by many Japanese.

Bibliography

Documents

Records of the U.S. Air Force XXI Bomber Command, Maxwell U.S. Air Force Base, Alabama.

Books

Coffey, Thomas M. *Iron Eagle: The Turbulent Life of General Curtis LeMay.* New York: Crown, 1986.

Fusa , Tsudori. *Kobe Kuushuu Taiken Ki.* (Account of the Kobe air raids.) Kobe: Nikko Shuppansha, 1965.

Hall, R. Cargill, ed. *Case Studies in Strategic Bombardment.* Washington, D.C.: Air Force History and Museums Program, 1998.

Hiratsuka, Masao. *Beigun ga kiroku shita, Nihon Kuushuu.* (American records of the air raids on Japan.) Tokyo: Soushisha, 1995.

Hoyt, Edwin P. *Japan's War.* New York: McGraw Hill, 1986.

———. *The Night Tokyo Burned.* New York: St. Martin's Press, 1987.

Koya, Aoki. *Inochi no hi wo tsuzukete.* (The day life continued.) Tokyo: Aogana Shuppansha, 1974.

Kobayashi, Keizaburo. *Senka ni Ikita Chichi Haha tachi.* (Parents who survived during the war.) Tokyo: Taihei Shuppansha, 1972.

Koyama, Hitoshi. *Osaka Dai Kuushuu.* (The great Osaka air raids.) Osaka: Toufu Shuppan, 1985

Kubota, Shigeru. *Tokyo Dai Kuushuu Kyuugo Taicho No Kiroku.* (The great Tokyo air raid, from the records of the chief of the rescue corps.) Tokyo: Ushio Shuppansha, 1973.

Kurashino, Techo, ed. *Senso Chu no Kurashino Kirokuo.* (Records of lives during the war.) Tokyo: Kurashi no Techosha, 1976.

Manabe, Motoyuki. *Tokyo Dai Kuushuu.* (Great Tokyo air raids.) Tokyo: Kokudo Sha, 1976.

———. *Honou to Kyoufu no Kiroku*. (The records of inferno and fright.) Tokyo: Kokudo Sha, 1976.

Morrison, Wilbur H. *Point of No Return: The Story of the U.S. 20th Air Force*. New York: Time Books, 1979.

Alldredge, Jennifer. *Toranku no naka no Nihon*. (Japan 1945: Images from the trunk.) Tokyo: Shougakukan, 1995.

Okuzumi, Yoshishige. *Chushotoshi Kuushuu*. (Middle-sized and small cities air raids.) Tokyo: Sanseido, 1988.

Saotome, Katsumoto. *Haha to Ko de Miru. Tokyo Dai Kuushuu*. (Mothers and children in the great Tokyo air raid.) Tokyo: Heibunsha, 1983.

Yamamura, Motoki. *Senso Kyohi Juichi nin no Nihon jin*. (Eleven Japanese people who refused to serve in the Japanese Army.) Tokyo: Shobunsha, 1987.

Index

About the Author

Edwin P. Hoyt is the author of more than one hundred published books, many of them about the Pacific War. He has long believed that the American firebombing of Japan was a criminal act, followed by the unnecessary dropping of two atomic bombs on Japan. He and his wife, Hiroko, divide their time between homes in Ome, a suburb of Tokyo, and Beaverton, Oregon.